Catz

René Kural

Catz

St Catherine's College
by Arne Jacobsen

With photographs by
Rasmus Hjortshøj

Preface – 9

Catz in the context of the book – 12

Plan of Catz with extensions and immediate surroundings – 12

I   *Prologue – 14*

II   *Inspiration and exchanges – 32*

III   *A stranger comes to town – 42*

IV   *Lovelace College – 68*

V   *St Catherine's layout – 78*

VI   *Lolita Motel: Hopes and expectations – 156*

VII   *The other Catz – 186*

VIII   *The most Oxford of Oxford colleges – 200*

Archival materials – 214

Illustrations – 215

Literature – 216

TV and film – 217

Index – 218

About the author and the photographer – 220

Acknowledgements – 221

Preface

St Catherine's College is named after the Christian martyr Catherine of Alexandria, who was born around 287 CE. Catherine was sentenced to death for her devotion to her faith, and on 24 November 305, she was placed on a spiked breaking wheel, which miraculously shattered during her torture. It is this wheel that history student Biba Jones refers to in her comment about the college logo (see page 31). This Cretan icon carries the signature of Frantziskos Kavertzas and dates to the first half of the 17th century. The painting, egg tempera and gold on panel, measures 16.85 by 8.94 inches and was donated to St Catherine's College by Ben and Lee Sylvester.

ST CATHERINE'S COLLEGE, OXFORD

It is a bit of a shock to walk through 800 years of mellowed Oxford history, cross the Cherwell on a temporary bridge, negotiate a bridgehead of mud and builders' lorries and find yourself well into the second half of the twentieth century. A pleasant, stimulating shock.

These words describe *Daily Herald* reporter Tom Baistow's experience of struggling across the rough landscape of the construction site, in October 1963, and setting eyes on St Catherine's College for the first time.[1] He was stunned by the modernity of the buildings and their sharp departure from centuries of tradition. The same shock still echoes through Oxford to this day and contributes to a unique sense of fellowship among the students at the college. 'Love it or hate it', as they say. The college continues to divide opinion, but there is a symbiosis between the low, ultramodern buildings and the people who live and work here. The many contrasts made me curious, and I felt an urge to explore them in depth in order to grasp what is at play.

My desire to write this book about Arne Jacobsen's own favourite project, St Catherine's College in Oxford, arose the year after I had completed the book *The Town Hall at the Edge of the Forest* about Søllerød Town Hall, designed by Arne Jacobsen and Flemming Lassen. As I pored through original documents in the archives, I discovered new information about the process leading up to the project, unknown plans for future extensions, long-lost garden plans, internal discussions among politicians and advisors, bewildered civil servants, merciless criticism in the Danish press of the runaway budget, satirical cartoons and songs, helpful comments from fellow architects, passionate op-eds from local residents, and much, much more.[2] I was curious to see if I might make similar discoveries in researching St Catherine's College. Baistow's comment about the pleasant shock is from his original manuscript, which I uncovered in my archival research for this book about another Arne Jacobsen masterpiece, which was Grade 1 listed in 1994 – the same category as medieval cathedrals.

Since its official opening in 1964, St Catherine's College has been colloquially known as St Cath's, Cat's, St Catz, or simply Catz, and its alumni are generally referred to as Cats. The moniker tying past, present, and future together is Catz. This name marks the ageless connection between the first students, the current students, and the ones who will be living and studying here in the years to come.

When I began to collect information about St Catherine's College, I became aware that there is a similar level of passion and love for this enclave of buildings in Oxford on both sides of the North Sea. This meant that there were many 'cooks' with well-intentioned suggestions and expectations for this book. This passion for Catz made me worried that I would need to act as gatekeeper to all these diverse expectations.

Over breakfast in the Catz Dining Hall, I mentioned my concerns to Peter Denney, one of the project architects for the college. Peter's reply was sympathetic but clear: 'Make it your book'. No point in attempting to write a book weighed down by other people's expectations. Naturally, such a renowned work of architecture has been covered by other writers, but this would have to be my story, told in my style and voice. Thus, in my search for inspiration for the book, I have aimed for an alternative, creative, curious – and personal – approach.

For the older foundations, the development of St. Catherine's pointed out the route they would soon travel. In a sense, St. Catherine's role in Oxford was to be an initiator. It could not advertise the historic strengths of the older colleges; rather, it had to focus on new challenges.[3]

As the youngest and largest of the 32 colleges that make up the University of Oxford, St Catherine's is in a position to blaze new trails for others to follow. That is what makes this particular college so unique.

In order to satisfy my curiosity about the unofficial side of Catz, I spent almost two months living at the college among the students. Everyone who passed by the floor-to-ceiling windows of my flat, at a distance of five feet, would gaze in with sleepy morning eyes. As a special trick, I checked the reflections in the building across from mine to

---

1) Baistow, T. (1963, October). Untitled [Original manuscript for the *Daily Herald*]. (IIJ Box 9_6).

2) Kural, R. (2018). *The town hall at the edge of the forest: About Søllerød Town Hall designed by Arne Jacobsen and Flemming Lassen*. Forlaget Rhodos.

3) Soares, J. A. (1999). *The decline of privilege: The modernization of Oxford University* (p. 141). Stanford University Press.

On the windows of one of the flats, someone had written 'come over :)' in yellow sticky notes.

When daylight strikes the walls and the cruciform columns in the Dining Hall, the space takes on a sacral atmosphere, even though there is nothing sacral about its purpose.

see when someone was approaching, so I could then strike the right attitude. Some quickly looked away, embarrassed; others held my gaze.

On the windows of one of the opposite flats, someone had written 'come over :)' in yellow sticky notes, an open, welcoming, cheerful invitation that was characteristic of the mood at Catz. In the evening, especially during the weekends, I could hear the young women's delighted giggles and the young men's gruff-voiced jokes. It reminded me of the vivacity and vulnerability of youth and student life but also of the opportunities life offers.

In Oxford, all the students wear their college logo on the left side of their jacket, proudly displaying their pride of being part of a community, a collective identity, a college. The main focus of loyalty for any Oxford student is their college, rather than the university at large. This is because the college is also their home, the setting of their daily life. The college owns and controls its own property and forms a day-to-day community for both students and tutors. Most have a room at the college, and tutors provide instruction in their offices and take their meals with the students in the Dining Hall.[4]

For members of the Senior Common Room, breakfast is served at 8 am, lunch at 12:45 pm, afternoon tea at 2:45 pm, and High Table Dinner at 7:15 pm.

At mealtimes, the tutors wear black robes, and the students respectfully rise when they enter. After dinner, coffee and drinks are served in the Senior Common Room: an excellent chance to hear rumours and unknown stories. During these after-dinner talks, I learned that there are 42 strokes of the bell at 7:05 pm every day – and that no one knows why. I also heard about 'the Dirty Thirty' but not what the term referred to. Rumour had it that Jacobsen was in the middle of a divorce when he designed Catz and inflicted his own personal misery on the students by deliberately designing cramped flats with narrow single beds. I also learned that Catz had been the setting of several films.

Arne Jacobsen created many world-class buildings and functional designs. It must have been hard for him to pick a favourite among so many works of exceptional quality, but towards the end of his life, he did reveal that if he had to choose just one of his works above all the others, it would have to be St Catherine's College.[5] This was confirmed by his son, Johan Jacobsen, when he visited the college in October 1996 together with his wife and two of their friends,[6] and it was further corroborated in a conversation with Margaret Davies, a co-author of *Creating St Catherine's College*, who was present during Johan Jacobsen's visit. And finally, Jacobsen himself emphasised his unreserved love for Oxford in a conversation with Pierre Jeannerat in the *Daily Mail* on 28 October 1960: 'I think that Oxford is one of the most beautiful small towns I have ever seen, equal to anything in Italy'.[7]

In extension of this point, the then architecture critic of the Danish newspaper *B.T.*, Henrik Sten Møller, wrote in his obituary of Arne Jacobsen, 'I always felt that among all his works, Arne Jacobsen favoured St. Catherines College in Oxford, and he beamed with pride when, five years ago, he was made an honorary doctor of this, one of the world's most renowned universities. – In literature, no less, as he pointed out, since the university does not offer a doctorate in architecture'.[8]

Like Arne Jacobsen, I am Danish, but I live in a different century. Inevitably, I view the story and the architecture from the vantage point of a citizen of a Scandinavian welfare state. In practical terms, my background proved a great advantage, as it allowed me to read source texts in Danish, English, French, German, and, to some extent, Japanese.

René Kural

Gentofte, July 2024

---

[4] IIJ Box 1_2: *Notes on Oxford colleges* (unpublished), p. 1.

[5] Davies, M., & Davies, D. (1997). *Creating St Catherine's College* (p. 101). St Catherine's College.

[6] Thank-you note from Johan Jacobsen in the archives, see IIJ Box 8_the-architect-magazines-photographs-of-individuals-architectural-comment-later-correspondence-with-the-architect-s-family-new-blinds_2022-08-05_1704.

[7] Jeannerat, P. (1960, 28 October). Among Oxford spires: A new sardine tin. *Daily Mail*, 9–10. (IIJ Box 9_3).

[8] Henrik Sten Møller deviated from this polite tone when he described Jacobsen's works as 'international industrial architecture' (Møller, H. S. (1971, 25 March). Arne Jacobsen død midt i sit arbejde. *B.T.*, 4.).

Catz in the context of the book

This map illustrates all five phases in the development of St Catherine's College from 1960 to 2024. Catz is one of Oxford's most exceptional works of architecture. It is important to note that the new builds in phases 2–5 adhere to the consistent design from phase 1. The Punt House in the lower left corner is the last of Arne Jacobsen's works from 1970, barely a year before his untimely death on 24 March 1971.

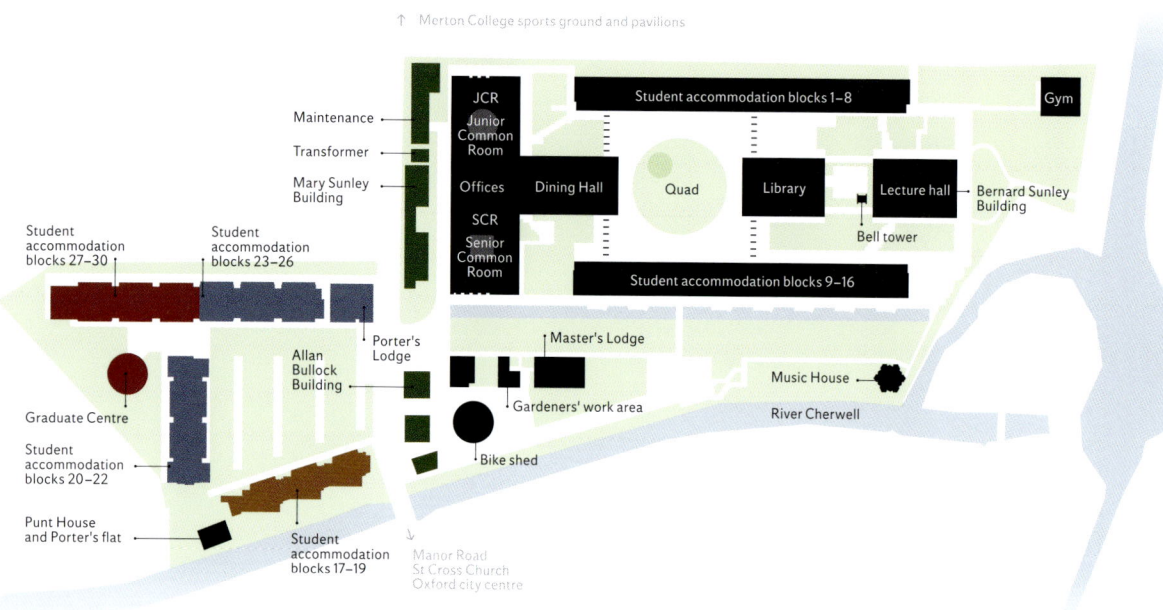

Phase 1	Phase 2	Phase 3	Phase 4	Phase 5
1960–1970	1982–1983	1995	2005	2021
Architect: Arne Jacobsen	Architect: Knud Holscher, Jack Lankester	Architect: Hodder Associates	Architect: Hodder Associates	Architect: Purcell

Catz is Oxford's youngest college. As such, its architecture marks the beginning of a process of stylistic, ethical, and economic renewal throughout Britain. This book is more than a description of the design of the building and grounds; it is also a story of the students who have been shaped by this place – for better or worse.

As it is told in this book, the story of Catz is not a chronologically progressing account. This is because the college is as significant today as it was when the first sketch was drawn. It may even be more significant, because so many young people have passed through the college and been influenced by its straight lines and the exuberant vegetation in the surrounding park. Some of the college's graduates went on to become world-renowned leaders, Nobel laureates, or athletes: Benazir Bhutto, former Prime Minister of Pakistan and the first female leader of a Muslim-majority country; John Ernest Walker, who was awarded the Nobel Prize in Chemistry; Joseph Heller, author of *Catch-22*; Jeanette Winterson, author of *Oranges Are Not the Only Fruit*; and David Hemery, Olympic triple medallist in athletics.[9] Others became good citizens and play an equally important role in the story of Catz.

The story skips back and forth between the present and the recent past. The book is deliberately cinematic in approach and editing. It is not a reference work but is intended to be read as a coherent narrative. 'Nova et Vetera', the new and the old, to quote Catz's motto – an apt reminder to have the most modern and the oldest disciplines go hand in hand.[10]

Today, the University of Oxford comprises 32 colleges, including St Catherine's. The oldest colleges were founded during the 12th century, their layout patterned on the structure of the ideal monastery, with an inner cloister surrounded by a church, accommodations, stables, kitchens, workshops, a brewery, an infirmary, and even a cemetery.[11] An autonomous community.

Naturally, the book places Catz into a familiar context but also illuminates the college through new, untold, forgotten, or neglected stories, drawings, and photos from both British and Danish sources. The book draws on original materials from institutional document and drawing archives, history books, scientific journals and reports, news stories, manuscripts, institutional memos, personal correspondence, alumni maga-

---

9) Stcatz.ox.ac.uk & Books LLC (2010). *Arne Jacobsen Buildings* (pp. 18–19). Books LLC.

10) St Catherine's College, Oxford. *St Catherine's College* (p. 30).

11) Here described based on the ideal Benedictine monastery, c.820. See de Wit, S. (2018). *Hidden landscapes: The metropolitan garden as a multi-sensory expression of place* (pp. 156–157). Architectura & Natura.

3–4 November 1958	7 January 1959	27 October 1960	4 November 1960	4 November 1960	5 November 1960
The Elevations and Choice of Architects Committee visits Denmark	Arne Jacobsen is offered the commission	The project is unveiled at Brown's Hotel, Mayfair	HM Queen Elizabeth II lays the foundation stone	The foundation stone is stolen	The foundation stone is returned

16 October 1964	26 October 1966	30 September 1982	14 February 1995	11 November 2005	8 August 2021
Official opening of St Catherine's College with Dining Hall by former Prime Minister Harold Macmillan	HRH Princess Margaret officially opens the Bernard Sunley Lecture Block	The Mary Sunley Building is officially opened	HRH Prince Philip officially opens the first section of newly built student accommodation	HRH Prince Philip officially opens the second section of newly built student accommodation	Master Kersti Borjars officially opens the third section of newly built student accommodation and the Graduate Centre

zines published by the college, transcripts of oral accounts, TV shows, film, personal recollections, and interviews. The architecture and life of the college are viewed through the lenses of film, literature, poetry, satire, music, critique, and recollections. The chapters are interspersed with interviews with Catz alumni, eight conversations in total with young people who are either students at or recent graduates from Catz. The interview questions are based on analyses of the recollections of students and tutors in the 2012 book *St Catherine's, Oxford: A Pen Portrait*[12] to make it possible to trace any parallels between their reflections then and the perspectives of today's students.

The interview questions relate mainly to the built environment.[13] The purpose is to gain insight into the relationships between the architecture and everyday student life at Catz. The format is a so-called biographical interview, which aims both to collect as many different individual perceptions of the place as possible and to classify common aspects across the responses. The interviews were carried out face to face in Oxford, Reading, and Copenhagen/Oxford (the latter pertaining to two interviews via Zoom). In a semi-structured format, all the respondents are asked the same set of five + one questions. The interviews were subsequently transcribed and edited for publication with the approval of the individual informants.

Interview questions:

1. *What were your first impressions when you first arrived at St Catherine's?*

2. *How does the architecture, design, or landscape affect you in your everyday life?*

3. *Is there a room, place, or section that is your favourite – or least favourite – location, and why?*

4. *If you had to use a metaphor for St Catherine's character, what would it be?*

5. *Can you describe an instance prompted by the physical setting, architecture, or environment of Catz that was particularly memorable to you?*

6. *Is there anything we haven't talked about that you would like to cover?*

The interviews are accompanied by recent student photos as illustrations of activities and people.

12) Ainsworth, R., & Howell, C. (Eds.) (2012). *St Catherine's, Oxford: A pen portrait* (pp. 160–189). Third Millennium Publishing.

13) The interviews are based on the method described in Ehlers, P., & Petersen, L. (Eds.). *Det kvalitative interview: Byens steder, borgere og brugere*. Realdania & Dansk Byplan.

I

Prologue

When St Catherine's Society was founded in 1868, the number of university students in Oxford was modest. From a social point of view, it is interesting to note that as early as the mid-19th century, Oxford and Cambridge universities admitted middle-class applicants of limited means as so-called non-collegiate students with the goal of providing less expensive access to higher education. Non-collegiate students were not attached to a college or provided with accommodation and were thus able to avoid paying the costly college fees.

In Oxford, this opportunity was used mainly by British middle-class students and by students from abroad, especially the United States, India, and Germany.[14] St Catherine's Society differed from other Oxford societies by offering a back door to college status for less privileged young men:

[I]t was the Oxford college for lower-class, state-school, science undergraduates. It was created by the efforts of social democrats and democratic elitists.[15]

14) Davies, M., & Davies, D. (1997). *Creating St Catherine's College* (pp. 1–8). St Catherine's College.

15) Soares, J. A. (1999). *The decline of privilege: The modernization of Oxford University* (p. 135). Stanford University Press.

The site as it looked at the time of Arne Jacobsen's first visit, in February 1959.

St Catherine's had no physical college.[16] The only thing that non-collegiate students could do was attend lectures and earn a degree. They felt like second-rate, if not third-rate, students at a very status-conscious university. They had no means or social standing. The same applied to the lecturers, who might come from other colleges and enjoyed none of the privileges or the special status normally afforded to British university scholars.

Eventually, St Catherine's Society was allocated a physical location: a single room in the Old Clarendon Building for tutors, administrative staff, and 26 students.[17] Unlike the other Oxford colleges, it offered no student accommodation. It is important to note that although the practice of living and taking one's meals at the university sprang in part from conservative ethics, it also contributed an element of culture and continuity:

> *From this perspective, the point to a university was not to provide just book learning and opportunities for research but also a social life that fostered tolerance and civility, where members of a college lived together, dined together, and participated in collective rituals that affirmed their sense of belonging to an old community.*[18]

It was not until 1936 that St Catherine's Society moved into its own facilities, a three-storey stone building on St Aldate's, south of Christ Church, with very basic lecture rooms. As it did not offer lodgings, most students regarded it mainly as an administrative hub.[19]

During the 1950s, students in other colleges referred to members of St Catherine's Society as 'Cats'.[20] After the war, from 1952 to 1956, St Catherine's delegates debated whether to transform the society into an independent college.[21] Among other benefits, a physical college would make it possible to provide bachelor students with accommodation. The society had outlived its original purpose from 1868, which was to provide education to students of limited means. By now, the gap between standard college fees and St Catherine's fees was minimal, and, moreover, there were scholarships available. The main problem was the lack of student places, and that could be addressed by founding a new college. The society itself did not have the funds that such a project would require, but money could be raised if the University of Oxford submitted the applications. The expected budget was £2 million, a considerable sum in 1956.[22]

Now came the challenge of finding a suitable location. Eventually, a rectangular plot on Holywell Great Meadow by the River Cherwell was acquired from Merton College. The area, eight acres of meadowland with poplars and willows, measured 800 by 400 feet and was situated on a north-south longitudinal axis.[23] It had become slightly raised during the 1930s, as it had been used as a municipal rubbish tip – mainly for bottles as well as tins and coal ash.[24] The setting was scenic but also close to Oxford's historical city centre: qualities that had a crucial impact on the design of the new college.

16) Bullock, A. *How St Catherine's College came to be founded* [A talk given to the Middle Common Room of St Catherine's College on 31 May 1984 by the Founding Master, Lord Bullock of Leafield; verbatim transcript]. (LXIC Box: Talks by Lord Bullock and others: Oral history).

17) Ainsworth, R., & Howell, C. (Eds.) (2012). *St Catherine's, Oxford: A pen portrait* (pp. 11–27). Third Millennium Publishing.

18) Soares, J. A. (1999). *The decline of privilege: The modernization of Oxford University* (p. 136). Stanford University Press.

19) Davies, M., & Davies, D. (1997). *Creating St Catherine's College* (p. 13). St Catherine's College.

20) Soares, J. A. (1999). *The decline of privilege: The modernization of Oxford University* (p. 145). Stanford University Press.

21) Trotman, R. R., & Garrett, E. J. K. (1962). *The non-collegiate students and St Catherine's Society 1868–1962* (pp. 48–60). Oxford University Press.

22) Bullock, A. *How St Catherine's College came to be founded* [A talk given to the Middle Common Room of St Catherine's College on 31 May 1984 by the Founding Master, Lord Bullock of Leafield; verbatim transcript] (p. 9). (LXIC Box: Talks by Lord Bullock and others: Oral history).

23) Zietzschmann, E. (1965). Saint Catherine's College in Oxford. *Bauen + Wohnen = Construction + habitation = Building + home: Internationale Zeitschrift*, (7), 283.

24) Margaret Davies talk for C20-Society-2002 Library architecture at Oxford-St Catherine's College (p. 7) (LXIC Box: *Talks by Lord Bullock and others. Oral history* 3); Juniper, B. The Gardens. In R. Ainsworth & C. Howell (Eds.) (2012). *St Catherine's, Oxford: A pen portrait* (p. 75). Third Millennium Publishing.

Raising the funds

The architecture in Oxford is highly homogeneous and dates back centuries, in part because the city remained nearly unscathed through the Second World War.

The book *Creating St Catherine's College* by Margaret and Derek Davies offers an in-depth account of the economic aspects of the college project until the mid-1960s.[25] The publication's focus is on the fundraising, how the site was chosen, how the buildings and the grounds were paid for, and so forth.

The general growth in prosperity and the establishment of an increasingly democratic society after the Second World War led to the founding of several new colleges, and the intended budget for St Catherine's exceeded the means of the national University Grants Committee. Another challenge was that while many foundations were keen to support the conservation and maintenance of historic buildings, far fewer were interested in supporting new builds. Thus, fundraising for the new college called for additional legwork and creativity.[26]

In spring 1958, St Catherine's Society learned that the future Churchill College in Cambridge was a competitor when it came to funding. This underscored the urgency, and after a meeting with a large number of industrial companies on 10 June 1958, the society had raised £675,000 and was on its way to reach the £2 million goal.

Churchill College was not just a competitor, however. The industrialists in charge of the Federation of British Industries felt that if the fund was going to approve a grant to Cambridge, they also had to provide funding to Oxford. Not necessarily a similar amount, but something.

Thus, appeals to corporate or family foundations, businesses, alumni, and other potential donors was not limited to Oxford itself:

> *The construction of St Catherine's is only possible thanks to donations from the Ford and Rockefeller Foundations, the pharmaceutical company Glaxo, the chemical company ICI, the detergent company Unilever, the insurance firm Lloyd's, the Barclays bank, the textile manufacturer Courtaulds, the oil companies BP, Esso and Shell, etc., in short, of all the flagships of the British and, in part, American economies.*[27]

From 1957 to 1963, close to £3 million were raised, with just 15% coming from British taxpayers. The bulk of the funding came from private business-owners in the United States and the United Kingdom with special veneration for Oxford.[28]

---

25) Davies, M., & Davies, D. (1997). *Creating St Catherine's College* (pp. 48–49). St Catherine's College.

26) Trotman, R. R., & Garrett, E. J. K. (1962). *The non-collegiate students and St Catherine's Society 1868–1962* (pp. 53–55). Oxford University Press.

27) Léger, J.-M. (2013). *Arne Jacobsen: Le College Ste Catherine à Oxford 1959–1964*. Moniteur Architecture AMC.

28) Soares, J. A. (1999). *The decline of privilege: The modernization of Oxford University* (p. 161). Stanford University Press.

Prologue

Alan Bullock

The inclusion of non-collegiate students had always been a key feature of St Catherine's and a deeply held priority for its leadership. Indeed, without this social aspiration, there would have been no college to write about today. In October 1952, Alan Bullock was appointed censor of St Catherine's Society, with the authority to make financial decisions. Over the coming years, like a real-life James Bond, he used charm, humour, and a degree of scholarly discipline in his fight to make the world a fairer place and keep the kingdom safe.

Alan Bullock came from modest circumstances,[29] as the son of a gardener and a maid. Given his background, higher education might not have seemed to be on the cards for him, as British academic enrolment had more to do with social class than with intelligence. The family moved to Bradford, where he won a place at Bradford Grammar School and later a five-year scholarship to Wadham College, Oxford. He graduated from Oxford University shortly before the outbreak of the Second World War. In 1945, he was appointed a modern history fellow at New College, one of the oldest Oxford colleges, and in 1952, as mentioned, he became the censor of St Catherine's.[30]

Bullock's own humble beginnings were probably part of the reason why, later in life, he would often intercede for students who were struggling financially by helping them apply for funds to be able to continue their studies at St Catherine's.

I have never told this story in public before, and on the whole, I think I never shall again.[31]

This reticent comment was made by the college's founder, Alan Bullock, on 31 May 1984 in St Catherine's Middle Common Room (MCR), the Bernard Sunley Building, and it now exists on two cassette tapes and in a transcription. His reluctance to tell the story stemmed from his feeling that autobiography and history do not go together. Especially if the narrator played a key role in events and might assign themselves greater significance than their actions warranted. At the time, Bullock had recently retired as master, 'because in a sense, I am a ghost'.

His speech – unpublished, as far as I have been able to ascertain – contains many anecdotes about the founding of the college, how he and the committee found their architect, the fundraising for the project, problems during the construction phase, and so forth. These and other recollections have been used to verify the story of the creation of St Catherine's in the following chapters.

Alan Bullock, the founder of Catz. 'Most students ride bikes, but one has a Bentley,' he said to the Daily Herald in October 1963 to illustrate how class divides would be reduced at the new college.

---

29) Spartacus-educational.com/HISbullock.htm (last accessed 3 March 2023).

30) In 1952, Bullock's acclaimed book *Hitler: A Study in Tyranny* came out. He continued this historical study of war in several later books, including *Hitler and Stalin: Parallel Lives* (1991), a bestseller that chronologically traced the lives of the two dictators – two tyrants who never met face to face.

31) Bullock, A. *How St Catherine's College came to be founded* [A talk given to the Middle Common Room of St Catherine's College on 31 May 1984 by the Founding Master, Lord Bullock of Leafield; verbatim transcript]. (LXIC Box: Talks by Lord Bullock and others: Oral history, pp. 1, 42–43).

Architect wanted: Searching for inspiration in the United States, Britain, and Denmark

Alan Bullock undertook two journeys to the United States in 1957, one on the ocean liner *Queen Mary*, which carried passengers across the North Atlantic until 1967. On his second tour, he was accompanied by six American architects. He studied the finest modern architecture in the United States, not just in the East and the Midwest but also on the West Coast. He was especially impressed with what he saw in California, but generally, he could not envision American architecture in a British context:[32]

> *It wasn't particularly relevant to what we were doing here because we had to create a college within the Oxford framework and the Oxford tradition.*[33]

He was not looking for an American architect but sought to 'educate myself and get my eye in'.[34]

St Catherine's established the oddly named 'Elevations and Choice of Architects Committee' headed by advisory architect Jack Lankester.[35] In a handwritten letter dated 12 June 1958, Lankester proposed an architectural design competition between eight or nine invited British architecture firms. Naturally, if Bullock already had the name of the architect he wanted, this would not be necessary. On behalf of the committee, Lankester expressed the hope that the design of the new college would break the tradition of repeating the styles of Oxford's existing colleges.[36]

An early Danish-British angle was proposed by Colin Boyne, editor of *The Architect's Journal*. He wrote to Bullock that, over dinner, he had noticed someone using the word 'masterpiece'. He stated categorically that this would not be possible, as there were no architects who could measure up to Christopher Wren, Nicholas Hawksmoor, or John Vanbrugh – great British architects, writers, and scientists from the mid-17th century. However, in the letter, he points to Stirrat Johnson-Marshall, a highly significant early reference to Danish-British exchanges in education architecture that had a crucial impact on the eventual choice of architect. Johnson-Marshall was responsible for the most remarkable accomplishment in post-war construction in the United Kingdom: the development of the national school building programme, which was a major source of inspiration for Danish architects' design of school buildings during the 1950s:

> *This is the one sphere of building in this country which has achieved international fame – not only because it has been designed from the 'inside out', in terms of children and teacher requirements for a good educational environment, but also because he has developed the use of new structural methods to supplement a traditional building industry suffering from post-war shortages of labour and materials.*[37]

After the war, Johnson-Marshall worked as deputy county architect in Hertfordshire and, from 1948, as chief architect in the Ministry of Education.[38] Bullock thanked him for the advice and apologised for his use of the word 'masterpiece', adding, 'I suppose everyone who builds a building wants it to be a masterpiece – and is a fool to put this'.

But Bullock did not want an architectural competition. He wanted to be engaged in a dialogue with the architect from day one, involved in shaping the ideas before they took on settled form. He wanted the project to be 'the architect's individual responsibility', not just one project among many others for a large, busy architecture firm.[39]

A majority of the committee members wanted to travel to Denmark. The very act of going on such a trip would offer a hint as to the eventual choice of architect, whether Danish or British. Both Bullock and Norman Fisher, head of the Staff College of the National Coal Board, felt that any shortcomings of the British construction industry were due to the low standards of the architecture profession:

> *To be a really good architect you need to be a thinker, to have high practical ability, to be able to manage other people, including some who are constantly out to frustrate you, and on top of all this, to be an artist as well.*[40]

The Danish Building Centre in Copenhagen and the Danish engineer Ove Arup in London helped put together a list of architects and firms whose works the committee could study based on photographs. The list included 29 of the leading architects of the time, among them Alison and Peter Smithson, James Stirling and James Gowan, and Powell & Moya.[41] Twenty-four were British, one was Danish-British (Ove Arup), and five were Danish. All were known for their post-war design, including furniture (John and Sylvia Reid). In England and Wales, the committee had inspected physical buildings by eight of the selected teams and by three other British firms (David du R Aberdeen, Yorke Rosenberg Mardall, and Denys Lasdun). The Danish candidates were the leading representatives of the field at the time: Arne Jacobsen, Jørn Utzon, Jørgen Bo and Vilhelm Wohlert, C. F. Møller, and Eva and Nils Koppel.

---

32) Davies, M. & Davies, D. (1997). *Creating St Catherine's College* (p. 59). St Catherine's College.
33) Bullock, A. *How St Catherine's College came to be founded* [A talk given to the Middle Common Room of St Catherine's College on 31 May 1984 by the Founding Master, Lord Bullock of Leafield; verbatim transcript]. LXIC: Talks by Lord Bullock and others: Oral history, p. 14.
34) IIJ Box 1_2: Bullock, A. *On being a client* (unpublished).
35) The paragraph is based on IIJ Box 1_The Architect-appointment-note by Lord Bullock – correspondence: 3_Correspondence on choice of architect, 1958; 4_Correspondence on choice of architect, 1959.
36) Trotman, R. R., & Garrett, E. J. K. (1962). *The non-collegiate students and St Catherine's Society 1868–1962* (p. 55). Oxford University Press.

37) Box 1_The Architect-appointment-note by Lord Bullock – correspondence: 3_Correspondence on choice of architect, 1958.
38) The Hertfordshire schools were the product of the County Architects Department led by C. H. Aslin.

39) IIJ Box 1_2: Bullock, A. *On being a client* (unpublished).
40) Box 1_The Architect-appointment-note by Lord Bullock – correspondence: 3_Correspondence on choice of architect, 1958: The Staff College of the National Coal Board, Principal Norman Fisher.
41) The archive contains many letters from patrons recommending their own favourites and from architects hoping to be considered for the commission.

This is a new idea, this is innovation[42]

The Munkegaard School. Jacobsen spent eight years working on the school, which officially opened in 1956. In interviews in the press, he called it his finest work to date. Watercolour, bird's-eye view from the south-west, October 1949.

The committee travelled to Denmark on 3–4 November 1958. The weather was inclement, rain falling from grey clouds. The Danish Building Centre had arranged meetings with the firms of C. F. Møller, who himself was away in Copenhagen, Jørn Utzon, who was away in Sydney, and Arne Jacobsen, who was in Paris until 9 November. With the principals out of town, the staff of the three studios had to step up. On a three-day tour, the committee saw works by five Danish architecture firms: C. F. Møller (Aarhus University), Jørn Utzon (Utzon's own home in Hellebæk), Vilhelm Wohlert (the Louisiana Museum of Modern Art north of Copenhagen), Eva and Nils Koppel (the restaurant Langelinie Pavilion), and Arne Jacobsen (the SAS Royal Hotel, Rødovre Town Hall, Aarhus City Hall, an office building for A. Jespersen & Søn, the terraced housing development in Søholm and the Munkegaard School).

The visitors were bowled over by the Munkegaard School. The chairman of the committee, Alan Bullock, summed up his impressions of the school:

> *I liked it at first sight. Scales, materials, and even planting in the courtyard were in perfect harmony. The children seemed to be in their own home. As I strolled through the elementary school, I was convinced that I had finally found the one that we had sought for two years.*[43]

Seven days later, the committee sent up white smoke. They had unanimously decided on an architect. Of all the buildings they had seen in Britain, the quality was too inconsistent for them to dare to hand any of them the assignment, whether to a young or an established firm: the latter, because high quality in one project that was due to the involvement of a talented lead architect was not guaranteed in another project. In Denmark, the committee had seen works of exceptionally high standards. They viewed Jacobsen's perfectionism and broad professional scope as a benefit:

> *Jacobsen [...] insists on controlling every aspect of the design of his buildings himself. The result is a homogeneity of design, which is very often lacking in the work of other architects. [...] He is versatile to a degree, his interests covering the design of furniture, wallpaper, lighting fittings, and landscape gardening.*[44]

In his report about the projects the committee had seen, both in Britain and abroad, subcommittee member and president of Trinity College A. L. P. Norrington was effusive in his praise of Arne Jacobsen's work:

> *Everything we saw had the stamp of mastery. This man never seems to put a foot wrong and shows great variety and adaptability to different sites and requirements. He seemed to me to equal or excel everybody else in all departments. [...] The care over details is something that other Danes show, but Jacobsen more so. He is especially good, also, at bringing his buildings (where this is possible) into relation with the surrounding soil by good planting.*[45]

---

42) Bullock, A. *How St Catherine's College came to be founded*. [A talk given to the Middle Common Room of St Catherine's College on 31 May 1984 by the Founding Master, Lord Bullock of Leafield; verbatim transcript]. (LXIC Box: Talks by Lord Bullock and others: Oral history, p. 20).

43) Suzuki, T. (2014). *Arne Jacobsen: Jacobsen no kenchiku to design* (p. 25). TOTO Publishing (TOTO LTD).

44) IIJ Box 1_The Architect-appointment-note by Lord Bullock – correspondence: 3_Correspondence on choice of architect, 1958.

45) IIJ Box 1_The Architect-appointment-note by Lord Bullock – correspondence: 4_Correspondence on choice of architect, 1959.

The architect is invited and accepts

Arne Jacobsen presents the drawings to Alan Bullock, and the two men inspect the site. Their correspondence clearly shows that they developed and maintained lifelong respect for one another and (almost always) refrained from questioning each other's competencies.

Towards the end of 1958, there had been some concern that handing the commission to a foreigner might lead to 'technical difficulties', not to mention indignation among British architects. In a meeting, Sir Basil Spence, the president of the Royal Institute of British Architects (RIBA), supported the choice. He argued that it was acceptable to choose a 'minor master', since no 'major masters' were available. Any bitterness among RIBA members could be ameliorated by finding a British firm to partner with Jacobsen. Sir Spence's positive stance should be seen in light of RIBA's plans to stage an exhibition of Jacobsen's works in February 1959 – the first solo exhibition by a foreign architect in the institute's 124-year history.

In a handwritten note, one of the participants in the meeting on 22 December 1958, when the Elevations and Choice of Architects Committee made their final decision on the choice of architect, summarised the decision concerning the final point on the agenda:

> *Get him over. See if he like (sic) him + he likes us. If Yes then continue the friendly dialo[gue].*[46]

The director of the Danish Building Centre, Kai Christensen, was briefed, and just before Christmas 1958, he was able to be the bearer of good news to Arne Jacobsen, who welcomed the news as an early Christmas gift. However, the thought of collaborating directly with a young British architect made him wary, since he had very personal ideas about architectural design.

Christensen reported back to the committee that Jacobsen was concerned that the need to accommodate a partner's preferences would constrain his design and diminish the quality of the work.

Just a week into the new year, on 7 January 1959, Maurice Bowra, the warden of Wadham College, who had taken part in the committee's visit to Denmark, officially offered Arne Jacobsen the contract:

> *I am writing, on behalf of the University of Oxford, to ask whether you would be interested in undertaking the design of the new college, which is to be established here with the title of St. Catherine's College.*

Bowra invited Jacobsen to Oxford to discuss the proposal outlined in the letter. He also brought up the need to bring in a British colleague, explaining that a local partner could relieve Jacobsen of the paperwork involved in securing the necessary permits and approvals from the City Planning Committee, the University Grants Committee, and the Royal Fine Art Commission.

Arne Jacobsen wrote back three days later to thank the committee for the trust they had placed in him. In this letter, he did not object to this aspect:

> *The collaboration with an English architect is of course necessary for you as well as for me, and I therefore agree to such a solution.*

The architect associated with the project was Philip Dowson, an assistant at Ove Arup. This was an ideal arrangement, since Dowson's was not just British but would also be able to draw on Arup's administrative and technical resources. At the same time, however, it was also a political and pragmatic decision designed to shape public perceptions.

Jacobsen arrived in Oxford on 15 February 1959, accompanied by his assistant Knud Holscher. On 18 February, he met with the committee. As the last of the 14 points on the agenda, the architect was asked whether he would be able to produce a plan or a small model of the Library proposals in time for a scheduled meeting in June with the philanthropic fund Isaac Wolfson Trustees, which since 1955 has awarded over £1 billion in grants to more than 14,000 projects all over the UK. Jacobsen accepted, with the proviso that he would be free to modify the design after doing more work on the general plans.

In autumn 1959, Dowson withdrew from the project. Even the original documents in the archives offer no clear indication of the cause, which suggests that his departure was based on a verbal agreement. The correspondence clearly reflects the committee's desire to keep their cards close to the vest in this regard, as it might reflect poorly on everyone involved in the project. Statements to the press explained that, during the summer holidays, Jacobsen had come so far in his work on the design that an associated architect was no longer required. Thus, no one else would be appointed to take Dowson's place.[47]

46) IIJ Box 1_The Architect-appointment-note by Lord Bullock – correspondence: 3_Correspondence on choice of architect, 1958.

47) IIJ Box 1_The Architect-appointment-note by Lord Bullock – correspondence: 4_Correspondence on choice of architect, 1959.

Villa Serbelloni by Lake Como

The wealthy American Rockefeller Foundation supported the initial planning stages for the new college and made the foundation's Italian mansion Villa Serbelloni available as a venue for the leadership's discussions about the future college.

Bullock had found his architect and the modern architectural expression he wanted for St Catherine's, but at this time, in the early 1960s, the new college was facing profound changes in student life. After the Second World War, universities were seeing an unprecedented number of applications, both from former soldiers seeking civilian education and, later, from the baby boomers who had just finished grammar school by the early 1960s. It was time to debate new teaching methods, the rift between science and the humanities (the so-called Snow gap, named after C. P. Snow's famous essay 'The Two Cultures' (1959) on the divide between literary intellectuals at one pole and scientists at the other[48]), the balance between research and teaching, enrolment policies and procedures, undergraduates and their problems (financial, social, security, relationship with tutors and so forth), arrangements for internal and external graduates seeking continuing education, the best use of the 28 weeks of term breaks per year, and – perhaps most importantly – an open discussion of the college's structure.

These general topics from the discussion are mentioned here because they were on the agenda of the meeting where the future of the college was outlined.[49] The American Rockefeller Foundation had contributed to the operating costs of a planning office for the new college, but that was the limit of the foundation's generosity. However, it did offer to sponsor a leadership seminar at its Italian mansion, the Villa Serbelloni. As the progressive leader that he was, Bullock invited the entire leadership team, with their spouses, to come to the villa in the beautiful town of Bellagio on the shores of Lake Como, north of Milan. On 5 April 1961, 26 people travelled to northern Italy where they spent the following ten days shaping the future of St Catherine's College.

The general discussions show that the team was open to critiquing its own actions and procedures. Socioeconomic changes and challenges were key topics of debate. The position of the university in society had changed: while it used to be the reserve of a gifted and wealthy elite, it was now becoming a place for the many. A high number of graduates still went into public administration, but the majority had careers in trade and industry. With this in mind, did the teaching methods need to change? Were they still designed to cater to the elite while the rest were left behind?

Another question was whether Oxford and Cambridge would retain their joint monopoly on world-class academic status in Britain and thus be able to attract the best and the brightest and deliver the finest minds to the most coveted and prestigious jobs. The seminar attendants differed in their assessments of the strength of the position of the two universities and the likelihood of any interventions to change it.

At the meeting, it was pointed out that the academic position of Oxford and Cambridge was complicated – and possibly compromised – by the social prestige associated with them. The leaders also highlighted the importance of appreciating human qualities, since anyone who participated actively in college life was not just an asset for the institution but also a valuable member of society and an attractive member of the work force.

This holistic view of the students led to an engaged debate about bridging the gap between science and the humanities. The problem was specialization, the one-sided focus on science or on literature, music, and the visual arts:

> *A university is a place where people learn to think, not to feel. If aesthetic enjoyment were their object they would do best to stay away.*[50]

In the final debate, there was broad consensus to support experimentation. Students should be encouraged to take an interest in other subjects besides their major; this should not necessarily be left up to the students' own initiative but should be actively promoted and, if necessary, arranged by the college.

The closing debates also focused on the students and any financial, social, academic, and mental health challenges and on their relationships with each other and the tutors. Expectations for the architecture were sky-high. The college, which was still under construction at this point, was believed to be able to build human relations by bridging the gaps between subject areas, social backgrounds, and past and future.

---

48) 'Between the two a gulf of mutual incomprehension – sometimes (particularly among the young) hostility and dislike, but most of all lack of understanding. They have a curious distorted image of each other.' Snow, C. P. (1959). *The two cultures and the scientific revolution* (p. 4). The Syndics of the Cambridge University Press.

49) IIC Box 6 Villa Serbelloni.

50) IIC Box 6 Villa Serbelloni. 6_Conference, p. 13.

The beauty of repetition is clearly manifested in the exposed columns and girders, like a whale skeleton on a beach.

Most students ride bikes, but one has a Bentley

Two and a half years later, in October 1963, surrounded by the noise of compressors and concrete mixers on the building site, Bullock once again commented on the vision of bringing science and the humanities together and healing the class divides in British education. Half of the students at Catz came from grammar schools and a third from top public schools, but there was also room for the more 'obscure' state schools that Oxford did not normally have any time for. Class divides were still obvious and reflected in the fact that while most students had bicycles, one had a Bentley. While puffing on his pipe, Bullock expanded on his worldview in an interview with the *Daily Herald*:

If we want to live in the twentieth century, we must have an education more in keeping with the problems of the age. I want a classless society in this college.[51]

He and his colleagues wanted to activate untapped talent, regardless of any 'accidental handicaps of birth and background'. To do this, they wanted to provide the best possible setting:

The influence of buildings on people is not properly understood.

Thus, his dogged search for a truly gifted architect made good sense.

51) IIJ Complete, Box 9_The Architect-Press cuttings_6: Manuscript for article by Tom Baistow.

Prologue

Catz moments / Antonio Gato, student of French and Spanish

I arrived at St Catherine's in a pram

Biba Jones, History

Biba Jones on the right in the pram, calmly asleep and unaware of what adventures awaited later in life.

6
It feels strange that we have a torture device as our logo.

What were your first impressions when you first arrived at St Catherine's?

I first arrived at St Catherine's in a pram, asleep and very much not interested in the college. My parents had come to look around Catz, and I evidently found it to be a very peaceful and somnolent place, because I fell asleep straight away. Funnily enough, when I arrived at Catz again 17 years later for the open day, my first impression was definitely a sense of calm and tranquillity, which must have been muscle memory… But also, to come from the centre of town with its tall, crammed colleges and hectic crowds makes Catz feel very calm in comparison. In Catz, the buildings are lower, and there's a lot of greenery and nature. It was only after I got my place at Catz that my parents found that photograph, and it was a funny coincidence to have the same reaction to Catz twice; only, the second time, I managed to stay awake long enough to have a proper look around.

How does the architecture, design, or landscape affect you in your everyday life?

I think living an undergraduate life in a building that is so intensely organised and uniform is quite ironic. It's kind of the antithesis to undergraduate chaos. Your room might be a mess, but all your furniture matches, and you might be running late for a class, but you're running across a perfect grid. There's a limit to how disorganised your life can be in Catz, because the architect has created a space that is so precise in its continuity and so controlled to the smallest degree.

Is there a room, place, or section that is your favourite – or least favourite – location, and why?

I think my favourite location in Catz is a spot just outside the door to the gym, where, from all the way across the other side of the quad, maybe 150 or 200 metres away, you have a perfect line of vision to the dart board through a JCR [Junior Common Room] window. I don't think Arne Jacobsen necessarily intended that, but it still feels like you're being dared to take the shot. As if some students could go into the gym to improve their arm strength, and then, as they leave, throw a dart 200 metres and hit the board. It also feels like a reminder that you're living on a grid, and that all the points in college connect.

If you had to use a metaphor for St Catherine's character, what would it be?

It's hard to think of a metaphor for Catz because of how distinctive it is. Lots of people compare colleges to monasteries, and I think that works for Catz. Maybe even more, it's like sitting on a train where the seat fabric, the handrails, the floors, and the ceiling are all the same colour, but because the view outside is so exciting and interesting you don't even notice the uniformity. Instead, it just adds calm to your journey and a nice contrast from the flashy changing view.

Can you describe an instance prompted by the physical setting, architecture, or environment of Catz that was particularly memorable to you?

It would probably be during my interview. The History interviews take place in the old quad buildings where the accommodation and tutors' offices are. There are gaps between each stair on the staircases that Jacobsen designed there, I'm not sure what the technical word for that is. Either way, the boy who did his interview before me wanted to intimidate me and throw me off my guard, and from across the corridor, he used the gap in the stairs to pull strange faces at me and do a kind of sarcastic thumbs up. All I could see through the gaps between the stairs was the faces he was pulling and his two thumbs. In a corridor designed differently, I would have just seen the stairs. But Arne Jacobsen, I guess, wanted the light to come through the stairs, and he wasn't accounting for the interview dynamics of how that might be used as a tool for intimidation. I actually never saw that boy again. But luckily, I wasn't intimidated and I got in, so I could spend my first year appreciating the amount of light that the old quad building lets in through those stairs!

Is there anything that we haven't talked about that you would like to share?

Possibly the only thing I'd change about Catz is the logo. It feels strange that we have a torture device as our logo. Quite a sombre design for a college tee! It feels like the more important part of St Catherine's story is the wheel shattering, and it would be cool to have a logo that shows that, like Tom Phillips' designs for the college [tapestries in the Dining Hall]. I think that would be a lot more exciting and probably more reflective of the vibe of the college!

Inspiration and exchanges

In the construction system, it is difficult to tell the load-bearing from the borne elements.

As Jacobsen saw it, municipal primary and lower secondary school should be an important setting of social development and preparations for life. It should not be a 'prison'.

It is clear from Bullock's comments about his initial impressions of the Munkegaard School that what he fell for was the democratic and humanistic educational approach that the buildings support and encourage. That was what they wanted for St Catherine's: a new agenda for young students in a new time.

When he designed the Munkegaard School, Jacobsen's goal had been to make every student feel at home and valued. As a child, Jacobsen hated school.[52] Just thinking about that time gave him chills. Now the time was ripe to focus on the needs of individual students. This was achieved through variations in landscape, paving, and recurring features designed to give each form a sense of having an independent and valuable existence. As Jacobsen saw it, municipal primary and lower secondary school should be an important setting of social development and preparation for life. It should not be a 'prison'.

In a comment on the connections between Jacobsen's work and architecture in other European nations, architecture historian Jørgen Sestoft highlighted the Nordic region, arguing that Europe could be divided into 'North and South according to the boundary between Catholic and Protestant areas'.[53]

This distinction brought much of Germany into the northern family, which made sense, since the neighbouring countries had obviously inspired each other across the border throughout history. During the 1930s, the Nordic region was insulated from the economic crisis, totalitarian regimes, and political unrest to the south, and developed a more informal and democratic architecture that might be described as Functional Traditionalism.

Jacobsen's postwar style had an international outlook and was a perfect match for his Oxford clients' expectations that the architect would apply 'the idiom of the contemporary style'.[54] Sestoft viewed Jacobsen's postwar works as the beginnings of what eventually became internationally known as Nordic Modernism:

It was almost tautological, if anything, to describe Arne Jacobsen's architecture as Nordic, for it was his works, among others, that defined what should be understood by that.[55]

52) Russell, J. (1964, 26 July). The Master Builder. *The Sunday Times*, 7.

53) Sestoft, J. (1991). Arne Jacobsen and the Nordic aspect. In Heath, D. (Ed.) *Arne Jacobsen 1902–71* (p. 53). Dansk Arkitektur og Byggeeksport Center, Gammel Dok.

54) Trotman, R. R., & Garrett, E. J. K. (1962). *The non-collegiate students and St Catherine's Society 1868–1962* (p. 56). Oxford University Press.

55) Sestoft, J. (1991). Arne Jacobsen and the Nordic aspect. In Heath, D. (Ed.) *Arne Jacobsen 1902–71* (p. 56). Dansk Arkitektur og Byggeeksport Center, Gammel Dok.

Architectural connections between Danish and British schools

That Bullock and his colleagues fell for the open-plan format of the Munkegaard School was no coincidence. In their design of preschools from the 1940s to the late 1960s, Danish architects and planners had found inspiration in Britain and Sweden. It was especially important to provide a welcoming setting to preschoolers, given the growing emphasis on levelling individual differences in academic attainment through architecture and furnishings.[56] Both in Denmark and Britain, the postwar baby boom led to a boom in the construction of new schools in the cities during the 1950s, as more and more people moved from country to city.

> *In England, the open-plan concept had begun to gain prominence shortly after 1950. While in the United States, this was driven by a shortage of teachers, in Britain, the motivation was a lack of school space. [...] This was further exacerbated by a shortage of trained labour and materials. Dual-purpose areas and the open-plan format allowed for a more rational utilisation of passage areas than in traditional school buildings.*[57]

In the 1950s, Danish schools were embracing new educational principles, focusing on both one-on-one and group-based learning. Schools were also supposed to fill a central role in community cultural life by providing a library, an assembly hall with a stage, multiple entrances, a public gym, close contact between home and school, and – perhaps most important – by having the teacher's desk placed directly on the floor, at the same level as the students' desks, rather than raised up on a podium.

These ambitions were reflected in a design of physical spaces that might raise the question of what came first – the open-plan solution or the educational approach?[58] The new schools were often designed as one-level structures characterised by quality materials, good detailing, bright and harmonious colours, individual desks and chairs that could be moved around, art on the walls or on the stage curtain, ample daylight, and experimental spaces that promoted new approaches in day-to-day educational practices.

Danish school architecture during the 1950s drew much inspiration from British school architecture, as described by Ning de Coninck-Smith with particular emphasis on the inspiration from Hertfordshire:

> *The single-storey British school buildings with plenty of light were very attractive to Danes, as was the attempt to work on an intimate and human scale that would enable young children not to feel lost.*[59]

British school architects had drawn inspiration from nurseries and their ambition that 'children's independence should be encouraged and their creativity stimulated'.[60] With its open-plan format and one-storey classroom pavilions with differentiated green courtyards, the Munkegaard School proved just such a setting when Bullock and his committee stopped by on a rainy day in November 1959.

---

56) de Coninck-Smith, N. (2010). Experts at work: A micro-study of architects and school buildings in Denmark, 1940–1970. In K. Petersen & Å. Lundqvist (Eds.), *In experts we trust: Knowledge, politics and bureaucracy in Nordic welfare states* (pp. 224, 240). Syddansk Universitetsforlag.

57) Kromann-Andersen, E. (1994). Åben-plan skoler – fortid og fremtid. *Uddannelseshistorie* (p. 80). Selskabet for Dansk Skolehistorie.

58) Ibid., pp. 82–83.

59) de Coninck-Smith, N. (2010). Experts at work: A micro-study of architects and school buildings in Denmark, 1940–1970. In K. Petersen & Å. Lundqvist (Eds.), *In experts we trust: Knowledge, politics and bureaucracy in Nordic welfare states* (pp. 239, 243). Syddansk Universitetsforlag.

60) Ibid., p. 239.

A modern-day fairy tale

When it opened in 1956, the Munkegaard School had cost 7 million kroner, which was described in the Danish press as an extravagant use of public funds. However, the architecture clearly promoted physical activity during breaks.

The Danish press was generally enthusiastic in its reviews of the Munkegaard School's departure from architectural tradition after the official opening on 6 October 1956, although some felt that the new so-called 'palatial schools' went too far. In a piece headlined 'Schoolchildren in luxury villas', the students were described as little princes and princesses.[61] According to the newspaper, *Aalborg Amtstidende*, this was not just excessive taxpayer-funded luxury, it was actually doing both children and parents a disservice:

How on earth are the former expected to feel at ease in their parents' modest home after being accustomed to spending the day in architect-designed settings? How are they supposed to be able to focus on their homework in the family home, without sound-proofed walls? Where a younger brother might be making noise, and the radio is playing. Letting our dear children live in the lap of luxury for one part of the day is doing them a disservice, since the rest of the day they need to get by as ordinary people, dealing with the harsh reality outside the school walls.

In North Jutland, Jacobsen's luxury school in Gentofte, north of Copenhagen, was viewed as an example of this unfortunate development. A modern-day fairy tale on a collision course with the humble conditions of postwar reality.

61) Skolebørn i luksusvillaer. (1965, 13 October). *Aalborg Amtstidende*, 4.

Catz moments / Bozhen Zhang, student of International Relations

A big empty swimming pool

Mia Campbell, Geography

In Catz, sitting or playing ball on the grass is allowed. Not all the tutors find these types of activities to be compatible with the respect owed to the central Quad.

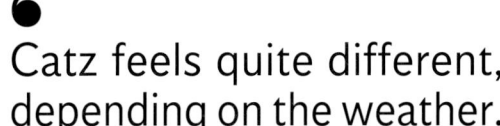

6
Catz feels quite different, depending on the weather.

What were your first impressions when you first arrived at St Catherine's?

I think the first time I came here would have been because my sister also came; she is three years above me. So it would have been coming with her to move in. And at that age, I wasn't sure if I would come to university. The idea of Oxford was quite intimidating, and I guess I held it up to a certain standard and expected a certain thing. I think I was probably quite intimidated by the college the first time I came, but I wasn't there thinking that I would ever go there myself. So, it was quite a distanced experience. I particularly remember the stream in Old Quad and thinking it was like this big moat to a castle. The big gates or doors were like this drawbridge. And I guess that now I walk past them every day, I never think of it like that anymore. It's a lot less scary and intimidating. But I remember the first time, holding it up to quite a high standing as an academic place. But when you live here every day, it becomes a lot more familiar and a lot less daunting.

How does the architecture, design, or landscape affect you in your everyday life?

Catz feels quite different, depending on the weather. On a sunny day, it's lovely, and the sun reflects off the concrete and glows lightly. And when there's a bright sunset, it reflects off the windows and looks really nice. The flowers are always lovely at this time of year. But equally, when you're here on a cold day in winter, and it's grey, it gets dark really early. It almost shapes your mood that day. I think when you walk out, the concrete can either amplify the feeling of sun and warmth, or it can amplify a cold grey, dark feeling. So it can shape your mood quite a lot.

I guess the layout of Catz encourages social interactions that are a bit more spontaneous. So having the big quad in the middle, you always walk and bump into people. Even though I've been in the Library a lot, you still bump into people and have a chat, which is nice.

This seems to facilitate quite a social aspect of college, because I do think Catz in general is one of the more social colleges.

Is there a room, place, or section that is your favourite – or least favourite – location, and why?

I found my least favourite easier to come up with, actually. There's a bit of the back of the Library on the ground floor that gets referred to as 'the dungeon', because when it's dark outside, it does feel very gloomy, and it's where people go when they have exams. So I avoid that as much as I can!

I don't know if this has come up with other people, but a great thing about Catz are these big windows that let the light in. The rooms are always well lit, but it also means that in summer, it's really hard to sleep. So I invested in this overpriced eye mask to help me sleep. Also, the beds! I don't know if people have mentioned how uncomfortable the beds are. But that doesn't help with sleep either. So that's probably my least favourite thing about Catz: sleep (or the lack of it).

If you had to use a metaphor for St Catherine's character, what would it be?

I found this quite a difficult question, so I asked a lot of people what they thought about this. But maybe, like, a big outdoor swimming pool. On either side of Old Quad, the Library and the hall act as the concrete edges. And in the middle, you have this space that's filled with life, I guess, like different experiences and social lives. But again, it links back to the thing about changes between seasons. In winter, you might drain the pool, it might be empty, and it's a less happy space. It feels quite grey. And then in summer, it becomes full of life again, with nature all around, and the sun reflects nicely off the water. So yeah, a big empty swimming pool!

Can you describe an instance prompted by the physical setting, architecture, or environment of Catz that was particularly memorable to you?

I remember when we finished our exams in first year, all the geographers came out of their separate staircases, and we all met on the quad, and everyone just sat there and chatted, excited that we had finished first year. I guess we also have some things in hall, like formal dinners with tutors or guests. For instance, every year, there's an event where you sit in hall and have dinner with your subject. And Geography get to sit at the high table in the hall, which is special, like, there's special cutlery which you get to use. And when you walk into the hall, all the other subjects have to stand up, which is quite funny.

Is there anything we haven't talked about that you would like to cover?

Maybe in terms of why I like Catz, compared to other colleges. I was at Worcester College yesterday, playing football. And it's got enormous gardens, it's beautiful, with so many flowers. It's a really nice college. But I was there with another girl from Catz, and we both said that what we liked about Catz is that you can actually sit on the grass. Whereas in a lot of Oxford colleges, they have these big barriers around their grass, saying 'Keep Off'. They cut it meticulously, with scissors, and like it to look really well kept. But I think there's something nice about having greenspace that you can actually sit on with other people. I think that's quite unique about Catz. Also, in terms of college football, I think Catz is great, because it has such a lovely community spirit, which means that even if everyone doesn't play sports, they come and watch to support.

III

Punchline

'For Heaven's sake, don't mention Danish architects!'

Both the British press and Jacobsen's colleagues in the Royal Institute of British Architects (RIBA) considered it scandalous that a contract of this magnitude and significance was handed to a foreigner. Why could the committee not simply have found a British architect among the 17,000 RIBA members? Or, if the goal was new architectural technology, why not choose one of the leading innovators – Le Corbusier, Walter Gropius, or Alvar Aalto?[62] A tsunami of scathing criticism poured from the pens, culminating in this public comment from Darcy Braddell, former Vice President of RIBA, in *The Times*:

> [This is] *the greatest slap in the face delivered to British architects since the Frenchman William of Sens was brought in to rebuild the choir of Canterbury Cathedral.*[63]

Ironically, Braddell's comparison of Jacobsen to William of Sens was actually high – if inadvertent – praise. The Frenchman who introduced the Gothic style to Britain was a famous and 'most subtle artisan' in church architecture when, in 1175, he was offered the task of rebuilding and expanding the burnt-out choir of Canterbury Cathedral.[64] So, yes, 850 years ago, Britain had invited an innovative and leading master-mason to restore the nation's first cathedral, but did it have to be a foreigner? In Cambridge, which had an architecture programme at the time, there were physical protests against this 'continental architect'.[65]

On 4 March 1959, under the headline 'Macabre demonstration against Arne Jacobsen', the Danish newspaper *Social-Demokraten* published a photo of students dressed in black who gathered around an altar and a black lacquered coffin upon which they placed altar candles 'in loving memory' of 'dear departed British architecture'.[66] They also laid wreaths with ribbons reading 'Here lieth British Architecture' and 'RIP'. Jacobsen and Holscher were unaware of this demonstration until they saw the Danish papers after their return from Oxford.

Every year, the *Architects' Journal* honoured individuals who, in the editors' opinion, had made significant contributions to architecture by naming them Men of the Year. In 1959, the Men of the Year were Alan Bullock and Arne Jacobsen.[67] At the time, however, no one had seen a single drawing or model. The announcement was made at a luncheon on 22 September. On this occasion, Bullock again pointed out that the architect was not chosen by him personally but by a committee. In a comment on the opposition to inviting a foreign architect to Britain, *Punch* magazine published a highly critical article titled 'The Catherine squeal: Should Danish architects be allowed to design Oxford colleges?' by B. A. Young.[68] *Punch* was a British magazine that combined humour with satirical drawings and engaged in debate with brisk and charming cheek. Referencing the many letters to the editor in *The Times*, the essay reminded its readers that architecture is art, and art is international. Young noted with astonishment that the Tate could buy a Picasso without offending local artists, just as the BBC could invite a foreign conductor to conduct a symphony with the full approval of the artist's British colleagues – but a new building? No, because a Picasso can be returned. A building, on the other hand, was for keeps, until it was either demolished or nuked.

> *I don't know who the leading English architects were in 1175, but I bet they didn't boycott William of Sens when he landed at Dover with all his newfangled Frenchified notions of how to build cathedrals. I think that once the language difficulty was solved they got together in corners and swapped ideas like mad.*

---

62) Harling, R. Was Professor Jacobsen's journey really necessary? (1959, 1 March). *The Sunday Times*, 33.
63) Braddell, D. (1959, 18 February). Why not a British architect? *The Times*, 11.
64) Britannica.com/biography/William-of-Sens
65) Makaber demonstration mod Arne Jacobsen. (1959, 4 March). *Social-Demokraten*, 3.
66) Ibid.
67) XL Box 10. *The Founding Master*; Box XL1: *The Founding Master*, newspaper article, unknown source.
68) Young, B. A. (1959, 4 March). The Catherine squeal: Should Danish architects be allowed to design Oxford colleges? *Punch*, 318–319.

'Trad' or 'Neo-University' and 'Mainstream' or 'Neo-Tech': According to the satirists, these are some of the rejected designs for St Catherine's.

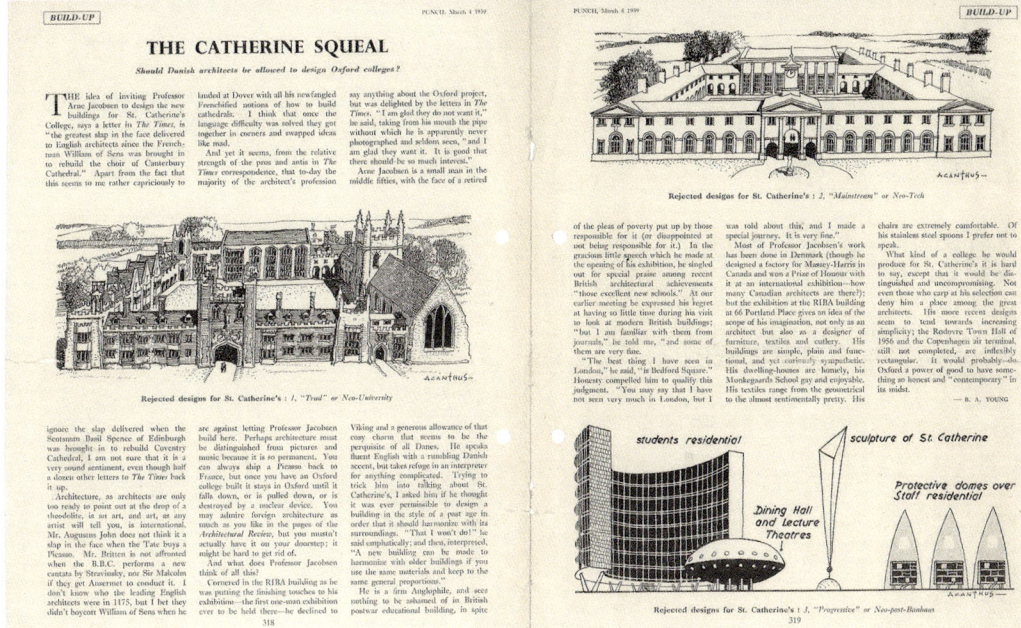

The author did, however, include a sarcastic comment about Jacobsen's cutlery design: 'Of his stainless steel spoons I prefer not to speak.'[69]

Bullock, for his part, was merciless in his assessment of British architecture in an interview with the student magazine *The Wheel*:

> *England has made notably few contributions to modern architecture and most of the major advances in style have come from abroad.*[70]

Later, in a private letter, he utterly rejected the notion that he owed any national considerations:

> *I do not think that nationalism should be allowed to dictate on questions of art. The one standard, surely, is excellence, and it is this that has led us to look elsewhere than at home.*[71]

In a 1966 review, a German architecture critic also did not mince their words:

> *In our century, at least, the English have been slow to embark on a modern development of architecture. They are really only getting to it now.*[72]

Punch illustrated their points with three sarcastic drawings of what a new college would look like if the standard approach to college architecture was applied to a new St Catherine's. Under the captions '"Trad" or Neo-University', '"Mainstream" or Neo-Tech', and '"Progressive" or neo-post-Bauhaus', the drawings pour biting sarcasm on contemporary projects that rely on tradition as their one and only direct source of design inspiration. The three featured project proposals were all presented as 'rejected designs'. The Danish architecture journal *Arkitekten* printed a casually ironic summary of the *Punch* article[73] with the attitude, 'why get all worked up, since the Brits are so perfectly capable of fighting amongst themselves?'

In yet another British defence of the Danish architect, the critic and journalist Robert Furneaux Jordan mused in *The Observer* on the problems associated with handing such a major commission to any of the ten best young architects in Britain, due to their limited experience:

> *Not one of them in 1959 can really show a body of experience and executed work such as would justify anyone in commissioning a college costing £2 million. A school here, a factory in Africa [...] a shop-front in Piccadilly – what is the use of that?*[74]

When Danish Vikings landed on the British Isles a thousand years earlier, they had a very different welcome, but then, of course, they did show up uninvited.

A foreign and inauthentic 'sardine tin' or 'tradition in modern clothing'? In a newspaper article titled 'The Founding Master', Bullock expanded on his (newfound) interest in architecture and on the vast effort that went into finding the right architect. During a three-week holiday in Denmark, he humbly declared that 'the client should remain silent'.[75] The client was required to find the right architect, explain the brief and otherwise keep his mouth shut: 'I don't think a building committee is capable of creating good architecture, so we don't interfere with the architect's work', he said.

Catz's archives contain his undated recollections (probably from 1959–1961) on the question about the client's role. Here, he tones down the client's significance in comparison to the architect's: 'Nothing else the client is called upon to do matters one tenth as much.'[76]

69) Ibid., 318–319; Ramaskriget om St. Catherine's College i Oxford. (1959). *Arkitekten*, 61(7), 128.

70) St Catherine's College. The censor interviewed by the editors of The Wheel. (1958–59). *The Wheel*, p. 4.

71) IIJ Box 1_The Architect-appointment-note by Lord Bullock – correspondence: 4_Correspondence on choice of architect, 1959.

72) Schulz, E. (1966, 30 July). St. Catherine's und andere Colleges: Traditionen in Beton. *Frankfurter Allgemeine Zeitung* (174).

73) Ramaskriget om St. Catherine's College i Oxford. (1959). *Arkitekten*, 61(7), 128–129.

74) Jordan, R. F. (1959, 8 March). Awakening of the Dons. *The Observer*, 18; Ramaskriget om St. Catherine's College i Oxford. (1959). *Arkitekten*, 61(7), 129.

75) (1961, 5 September). Bygherren skal holde sin mund. *Politiken*, 9.

76) IIJ Box 1_2: Bullock, A. *On being a client* (unpublished).

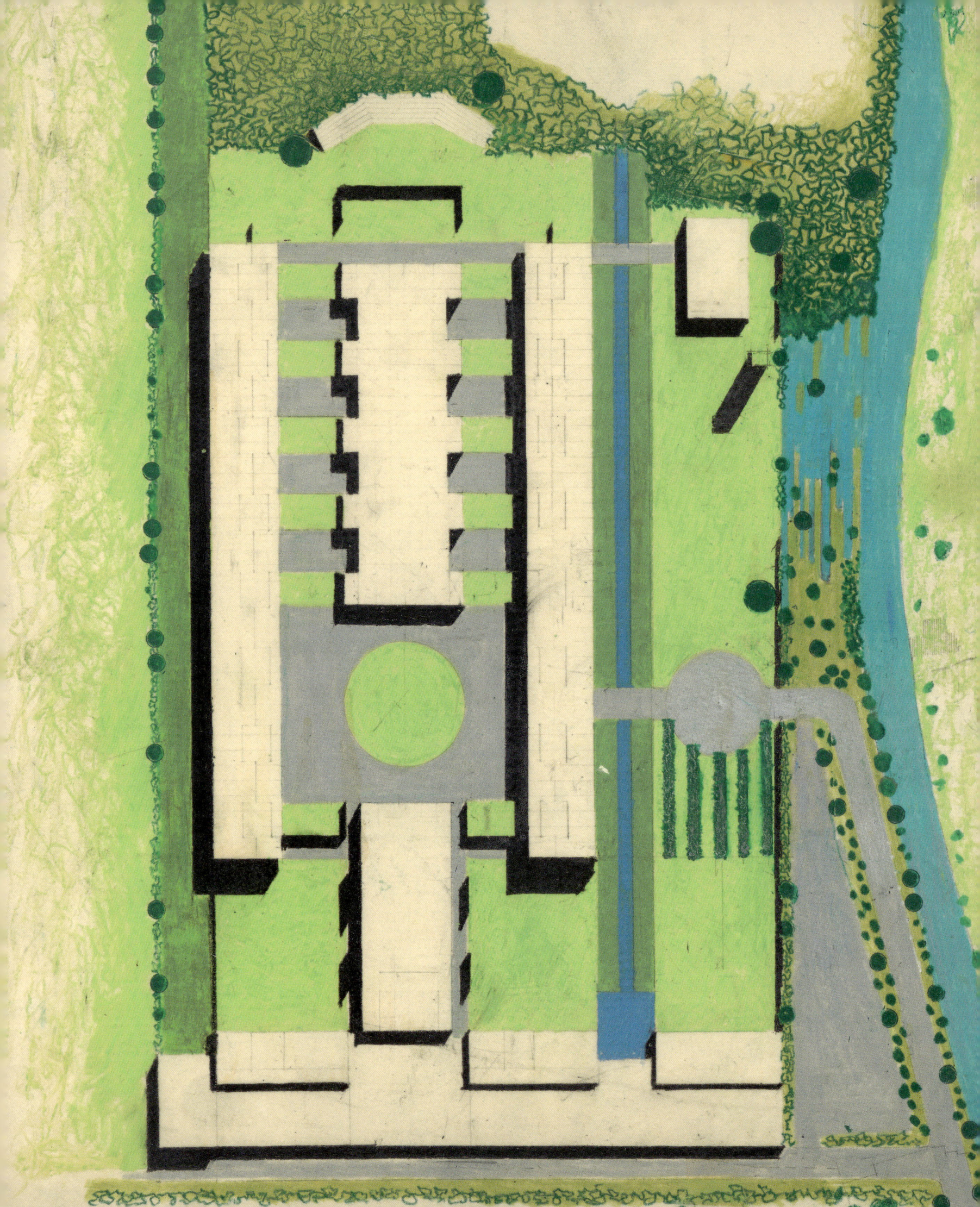

Early coloured site plan with the Master's house in the top right corner, where the Music House stands today. The ink and watercolour drawings in the archives were probably coloured by Arne Jacobsen himself, as he was a true master of this, as confirmed by Knud Holscher.

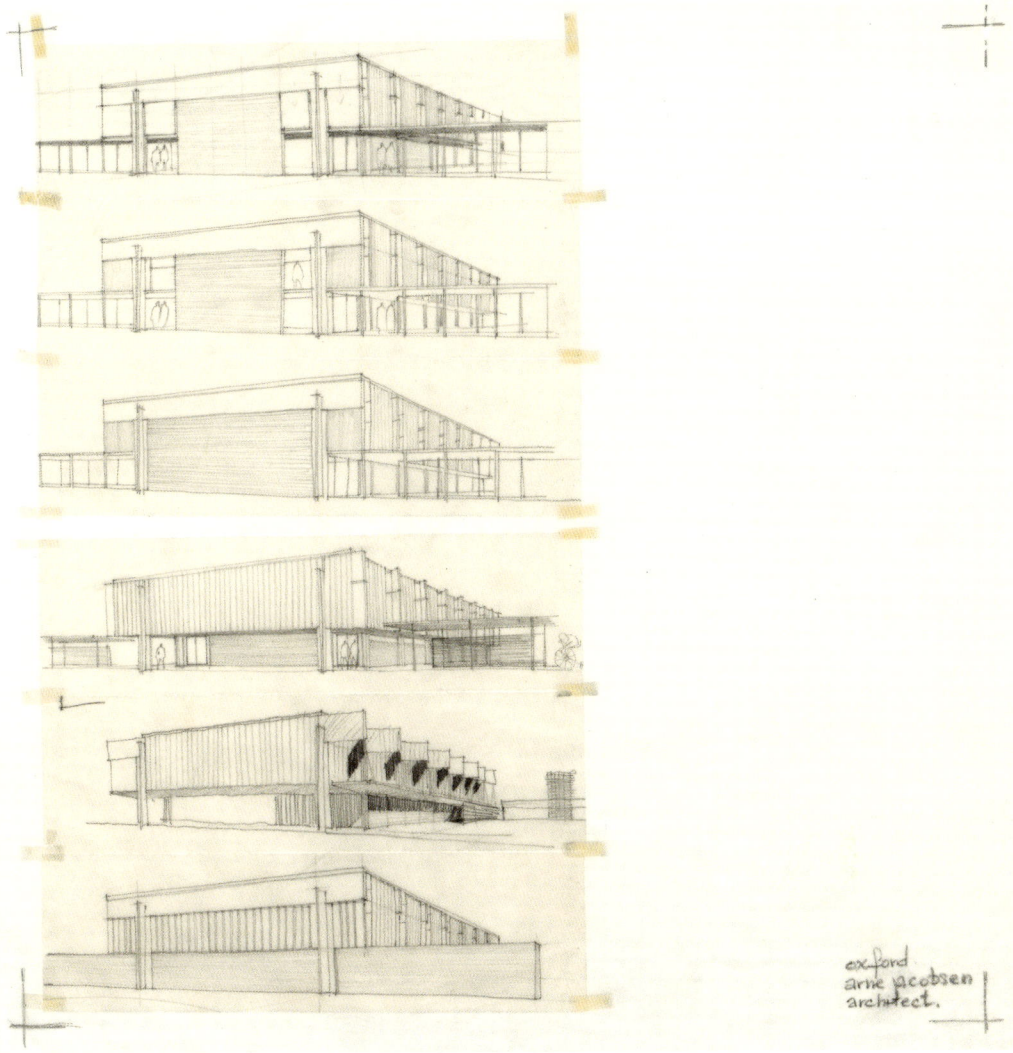

Studies of corners, facades, and constructions.

Thus, the architect should be given a free hand. And if the result did not live up to expectations: 'At least we shall have no one to blame but ourselves, and this is as high as any client should allow his ambitions to rise.'

After prolonged radio silence, Jacobsen finally rang Bullock and wanted to come to London, bringing models, drawings, and photographs. Bullock and Lankester were so excited about seeing the result that they drove to Heathrow Airport to meet him. They were not even out of the customs building before they pulled the model out of the wrapping: 'He got it right at the beginning.'[77] With a few minor changes, the current college reflects these early drafts.

When the architectural sketches were subsequently presented to the public at Brown's Hotel in Mayfair, in 1960, one of the scathing comments from the British press was that the buildings looked like 'a new sardine tin'.[78] Or like something 'foreign and inauthentic' that failed to capture the British spirit, as the 80-year-old Professor Sir Albert Richardson was quoted as saying to the *Daily Express*:[79] 'This building is a foreign thing – a stunt'.[80]

Even the critic from *The Builder*, a fellow architect, found the project disappointing: the general approach seemed overly simple and rigid, the low buildings of uniform height were monotonous, and the general treatment of the facades appeared dull. On second thoughts, however, he changed his mind.

Even though the proposal, as he saw it, was neither revolutionising or dramatic, he kindly predicted that in the future, the college would be regarded as 'a quiet, distinguished and scholarly group of buildings'.[81]

Oxford's existing colleges were dominated by aristocratic architecture – Gothic and Elizabethan styles from the 16th centuries and, later, Neo-Gothic and Neo-Elizabethan – and it was a very different architectural approach that characterised the late-modern plans for the new college.[82] The old colleges in Oxford had age, tradition, and reputation in their favour. A new college would have to create a name and reputation for itself, based on the quality of its archi-

77) Bullock, A. (1984). *How St Catherine's College came to be founded* [A talk given to the Middle Common Room of St Catherine's College on 31 May 1984 by the Founding Master, Lord Bullock of Leafield; verbatim transcript] (pp. 28–29). (LXIC Box: Talks by Lord Bullock and others: Oral history).

78) Jeannerat, P. (1960, 28 October). Among Oxford spires: A new sardine tin. *Daily Mail*, 9–10.

79) Møller, P. (1960, 28 October). Stormen blæser op mod Arne Jacobsen. *B.T.*, back page.

80) The old and mellow colleges of Oxford meet a long, low concrete stranger. (1960, October). *Daily Express*.

81) Booth, D. (1960). St Catherine's College, Oxford. *The Builder*, 118(6129), 821.

82) I use the term 'late modern', because it contains (according to Anthony Giddens) a 'detraditionalisation' in a shift away from handed-down customs and towards individual preferences.

tecture.[83] 'I wasn't trying to show Oxford how to live [...] I just wanted to translate the Oxford tradition into modern terms,' as Jacobsen humbly commented.[84]

The Danish architecture journal *Arkitekten* and parts of the general press in Denmark quoted five British newspapers' assessments of the project.[85] The review in *The Guardian* (28 October 1960) pointed in two directions, highlighting, on the one hand, the strength of expression and, on the other, the monotony of repetition:

This will be the most classical building ever built in Oxford. Shown to a necessarily small scale its strictly repeating columns tend to look dull.

The Times (28 October 1960) could not discern any typically Scandinavian feel nor any humour on the part of the architect but instead recognised the best aspects of contemporary American architecture and noted the similarity between the exterior design of the college and Jacobsen's new SAS building:

Instead of making warmth and charm his objectives, and informal landscaping and the use of natural timbers his means of achieving them, Professor Jacobsen has gone for discipline and a cold purity of form.

The ascetic modernity notwithstanding, the newspaper's critic still saw traces of the college cloister.

The *Daily Mail* (28 October 1960) saw the comfortable aspects of life as a sardine:

'The sardine tins have reached the City of Spires' is one sarcasm poured in my ear at the conference in Brown's Hotel, Mayfair, where we were shown a model, plans, and photographs of the future buildings, and where the Master of St. Catherine's, Mr. Alan Bullock, historian and TV personality, introduced the architect, Professor Arne Jacobsen, a Dane of world-wide fame.[86]

83) Carter, J. (1971, 17 November). *Architects' Journal Information Library*, p. 1106.

84) Russell, J. (1964, 26 July). The Master Builder. *The Sunday Times*, 8.

85) Sådan siger de andre. (1961). *Arkitekten*, 63(1), A 26, A 28; Dansk arkitekt bedømt i England (1961, 18 January). *Demokraten*, 4.

86) Jeannerat, P. (1960, 28 October). Among Oxford spires: A new sardine tin. *Daily Mail*, 9–10.

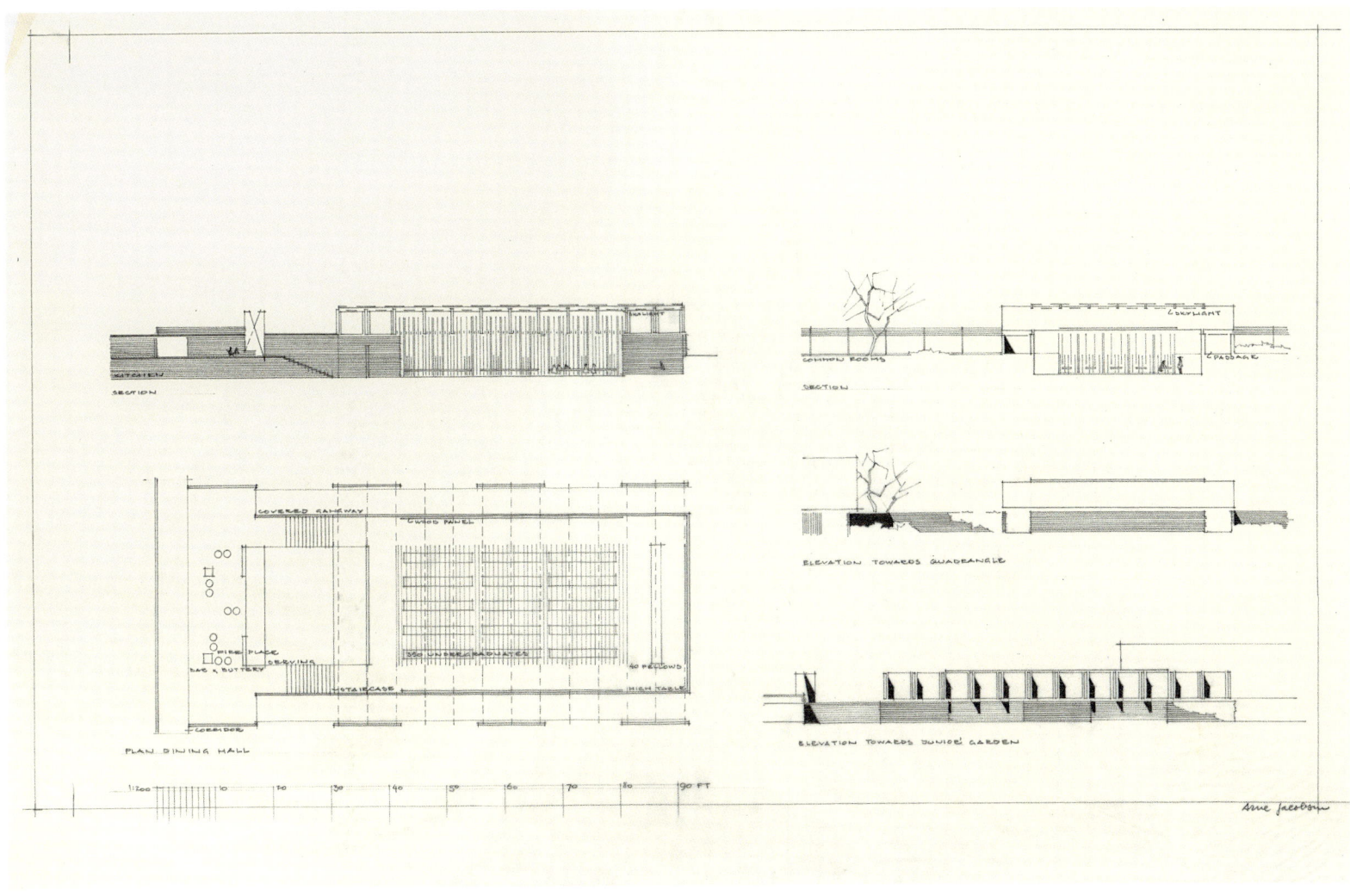

Perspective of the Quadrangle.

Section and plans of the Dining Hall.

In a feature article on the Dane, *The Sunday Times* attempted a conciliatory tone by dismissing the British protests as 'a mild cultural commotion, but it is clear from the text that the paper did not consider the then 58-year-old Jacobsen as a typical modern cosmopolitan:

> [He] *looks more like a farmer or one-time soccer player* [...] *He has a gentle, probing, unflurried manner* [...] *a reflective, occasionally even perplexed manner, a ready humour, and a deep humanity.*[87]

Their view of Jacobsen as a humanist owed in part to a certain emphasis on accessibility rather than high walls, which presented an obstacle to young university students returning home inebriated from a night out on the town and had to cover the broken glass on the top walls with their gowns, thus tearing the fabric. Jacobsen chose to omit walls, and to this day, St Catherine's is one of the only Oxford colleges that is not walled in.[88] This was not universally welcomed by the leadership. In letters to the dean in both 1962 and 1965, the Senior Proctor expressed his concern over the lack of enclosing walls, barbed wire, and spikes.[89] The police had recorded incidents of theft and noted that the offences largely ended at midnight, when most of the students had settled in for the night. The Senior Proctor argued that the extent of off-campus student life at night was directly proportional to the amount of trouble. Ultimately, however, St Catherine's remained an open college.

87) *The Sunday Times* (1960, 30 October), 9. (IIJ Box 9).

88) Nielsen, J. A. (1964, 24 July). Ikke en dansker, men Arne Jacobsen. *Politiken*, 10.

89) XIID Box. *Closure at night*.

The Danish press

In fairness, the characterisation of Jacobsen in the British press was not very different from how the architect was represented in parts of the Danish press:

> *As a person, he is profoundly modest. […] Professionally, he is ambitious, but as a person, he is rather unambitious.*[90]

Berlingske Tidende captured Jacobsen in his home as 'a happy boy' who offered an equally muted self-portrait:

> *There is absolutely nothing extraordinary about me. I may be an architect, but I am neither a philosopher, left-handed, nor in any sense a 'prima donnerd'.*[91]

This down-home image notwithstanding, in 1963, the newspaper *Aktuelt* included Jacobsen on its list of the 100 most influential Danes.

His design of St Catherine's College thus placed him alongside furniture designer Hans J. Wegner and the social critic, lighting designer, writer, and architect Poul Henningsen in a company otherwise dominated by business leaders, ministers, heads of trade associations, directors general, and potential future prime ministers.[92]

Throughout his career, the Danish press maintained a fluctuating love-hate relationship with Jacobsen. As early as in February and April 1959, there seemed to be a certain consternation over the British architecture profession's concerted letter-writing campaign against the Danish professor and the compromise solution of including the English architect Philip Dowson as a local project partner.[93] The newspaper *Politiken* considered it absurd that British architects would want to want to pass over a fellow colleague simply because he was Danish and pointed to the transfusion of fresh blood that outside contributions had historically represented in both British and Danish architecture and visual art.

---

90) Dr. Jacobsen, I presume. (1968, 2 February). *Berlingske Tidende*, back page.
91) Mentze, E. (1959, 19 April). Teknik og aandfuldt haandværk samles i St. Catherine's College. *Berlingske Tidende*, 17.
92) Malmquist, O. (1963, 5 December). 100 på toppen. *Aktuelt*, 18.
93) Arkitekt-kampagne mod Arne Jacobsen. (1959, 25 February). *Politiken*, 5; 11; Arne Jacobsen accepterer. (1959, 7 April). *Politiken*, 12.

Dying for a smoke

In a piece in B.T. on 27 February 1959, cartoonist Mogens Juhl commented on the British architects' attacks on Jacobsen. With reference to Jacobsen's famous Egg and Swan chairs, the bullying took place in a chicken run: 'He's too big and strange, and therefore he needs a good whacking.' The drawing is a good example of the sympathy he met in his native country.

On 22 June 1966, as the first architect ever, Jacobsen was awarded an honorary doctorate in literature (DLitt) from the University of Oxford for his design of St Catherine's College. On this occasion, too, the Danish press was tremendously proud of their countryman. Even newspapers with a local or limited readership, such as *Hejmdal, Information, Holstebro Dagblad, Bornholmeren, Lollands Ny Dag,* and the Communist *Land og Folk* mentioned the honour.

At the ceremony, Jacobsen wore a red gown with grey bell-shaped silk sleeves and a black velvet cap. The diploma was presented by former British Prime Minister Harold Macmillan.

In his speech at the event, the main speaker, A. N. Bryan-Brown, mused in Latin on the Danish architect's constant habit of chewing on his pipe: '*Iam diu, opinor, a lituo fumivomo aegre abstinet*'. In the programme for the event, this was translated to 'But I'm sure he is dying for a smoke'.[94]

In closing, Bryan-Brown said,

Professor Jacobsen is a brilliant architect who can claim to have introduced a new style of architecture to Oxford and to have reversed the achievement of Augustus, making brick serve where stone were used before.

On Monday, 8 November 1965, Jacobsen was awarded RIBA's bronze medal for 'an outstanding example of modern architecture' as the second foreign architect ever,[95] and in March 1968, along with four others, he was awarded an honorary doctorate from the University of Strathclyde in Glasgow.[96]

94) *Encaenis Addresses*. The Danish National Archives (Business Archive). Minutes of meetings 1965, 1966 (280); Grigs, D. Encaenia in Oxford. (1966, 22 June). *Oxford Mail*, frontpage;

95) In a letter to engineer Poul Ahm, Ove Arup and Partners, Jacobsen writes: 'If I am awarded an actual medal, it ought to be cut into three pieces to be handed to those who earned it, including yourself.' Correspondence. St Catherine's College Oxford. The Danish National Archives (Business Archive). Correspondence 1965, 1968 (285).
96) Doctor of Laws (LLD) studylib.net/doc/6889892/honorary-graduates-university-of-strathclyde.

Queen Elizabeth II and Chancellor Harold Macmillan walking in procession to the Sheldonian Theatre in November 1960. Behind them on the left, Prince Philip, Duke of Edinburgh.

The foundation stone that disappeared

During the five-hour-long royal visit, Queen Elizabeth laid the foundation stone for St Catherine's College on Holywell Great Meadow. At the event, she expressed her delight that now, in 1960, a woman could engage in intellectual pursuits without jeopardising her chances of having a family. By this time, women's colleges in Oxford had the same status as men's colleges.

A lengthy effort to prepare the low-lying meadow on the banks of the River Cherwell preceded the event on 4 November 1960, when the Queen laid the foundation stone at the very spot where Master Alan Bullock would later sit in the Dining Hall.[97] The marshy area had been reclaimed during the war, and in the Danish press, it was estimated that the construction of the new college would cost approximately £2.3 million.[98]

The following day, *Politiken* and other Danish and British newspapers described how three students, under cover of night, had hoisted the stone up and carried it off on a wheelbarrow.

A local police officer on patrol had noticed the figures straining in the dark and arrested them for 'breaking the peace'. After an hour's questioning at the station, the matter was reported to the university, and the offending students were suspended.

Jacobsen was still in Oxford when this happened but was unperturbed. Saturday had been Guy Fawkes' Day,[99] or Bonfire Night,[100] and the university had prohibited the students from lighting bonfires, setting off fireworks, or engaging in other mischief. Unhappy about the ban, the students took matters into their own hands, held their own celebrations, and made away with 'the Queen's stone'.

The story was covered in many minor and major Danish newspapers. The three students, who came from South Africa and Britain, respectively, had to send a written apology before they were reinstated and could continue their studies. The stone was returned unscathed and is now – with some additional history – embedded in the wall behind High Table.

---

97) Arne Jacobsens Oxford. (1960, 28 October). *Politiken*, 1, 9; Elizabeth fik diskret hjælp da hun murede. (1960, 5 November). *Politiken*, 1, 2.

98) Kongelig begivenhed for Arne Jacobsen. (1960, 28 September). *Dagens Nyheder*; Englands dronning ser dansk arkitektur. (1960, 28 September). *Næstved Tidende*.

99) As the Danish website religion.dk notes, the alleged actions of a religious fanatic may also be seen as symbolic of a modern-day struggle for liberation in the world of art, perhaps because a true hero is always in opposition to established society. As national values are seen to erode, people may then turn to the traditional enemies of the state.

100) Oxford-grundstenen fjernet i trillebør af tre studerende. (1960, 6 November). *Politiken*, 4.

Foundation stone with the Master's Oxford chair.

A Dane comes to England

Even to a Brit, the structure of a college in Oxford or Cambridge can be difficult to grasp. When Jacobsen arrived in Oxford on 15 February 1959, his Scandinavian background made it all the harder. Universities in Oxford and Cambridge differed from other British institutions of higher learning on two key points: governance and educational approaches.[101]

In 1959, the University of Oxford was made up of 30 independent colleges, 25 for men and 5 for women, of which St Catherine's later became the largest. The colleges were financially independent and all had income from a number of sources, including landholdings, private foundations, contributions from alumni, student fees, and government grants. How this money was spent was entirely up to the individual college. The university received government grants but was entirely self-governing. It preserved its independence and was fully in charge of the allocation of funds to the colleges, which did not receive government grants directly but through the university only.

It was up to each college to decide whom and how many to accept in each field of study, just as all members of the teaching staff were appointed by the college leadership, which comprised the college's teaching members (tutors) and the head of the college. The latter was known under a variety of titles in the individual colleges: Master, Warden, Provost, Rector, or President. While colleges appointed their own teaching staff, the university appointed the professors, who considered the college their academic home. Tutors and professors gave lectures in their respective colleges, but these lectures were open to all Oxford students. Similarly, the university's laboratories were available to all colleges. Tuition was organised by the colleges, while examinations and the awarding of university degrees was handled by the university.

Naturally, each study subject determined its own teaching methods, but the common mainstay of instruction was one-on-one tutorials. Students met with their tutors weekly to receive comments and directions based on their work so far. This often fostered a close personal relationship. The tutor might recommend a student to take tutorials in a different college while still being responsible for the course as a whole and for structuring their student's work.

Tutorials were usually held in the lecturer's private office, where they kept their books and personal items. The personal bond was further enhanced by the fact that tutors and students lived in the same community. In addition to daily meals and special events, stage productions, concerts, games, sports, clubs, and so forth all helped to build a collective identity.

The college buildings contained rooms for all tutors and students. In Cambridge and Oxford, the colleges were residential. The vast majority of students lived in college, although some had accommodations in town but still enjoyed the full membership of college, took many of their meals there, used the library, and generally participated in college life. The Dining Hall was important, as this was where everyone had their meals, and every night, it formed the setting of a formal dinner. Colleges featured separate common rooms for the tutors (Senior Common Room, abbreviated to SCR) and students (Junior Common Room, abbreviated to JCR), the Master's house, gardens and sports facilities.

Traditionally, the rooms were accessed directly from staircases, rather than corridors, and were built around a rectangular lawn or as a block facing a garden. Oxford colleges handled their own purchases but were also part of a common purchasing arrangement.

101) This section is based mainly on material in IIJ Box 1_2: *Notes on Oxford Colleges* (unpublished).

Section perspective of student accommodation organised around the staircase.

Perspective of student accommodation facing the rectangular water garden with terraces running the full length of the west side of the area.

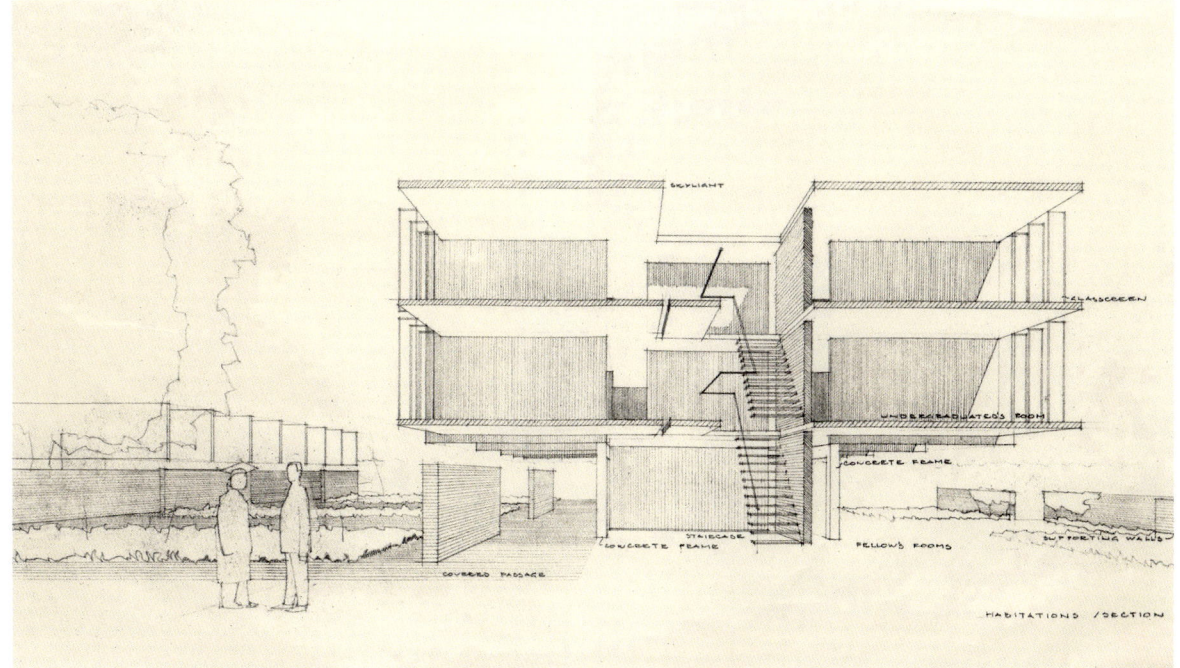

A stranger comes to town

Arne Jacobsen greets Prince Philip at the official opening in 1964. On the left, Alan Bullock. On 23 May, *Politiken* wrote that the Prince had slipped away from his entourage and nipped into the kitchen, where his appearance had caused quite a stir. He praised the architecture to Jacobsen and observed that the old traditions were beautifully preserved in the new forms.

New or old?

Jacobsen's wingman in England, Peter Denney, has explained that the design of St Catherine's College was not based on the old colleges in town, even though Jacobsen had visited both Cambridge and Oxford in his youth. Provided with plans of all the colleges in Oxford and Cambridge, he included traditional elements, such as the large open Quad and the choice of placing the student accommodation on the first floor around staircases.[102] In this way, the project reflects the dual task of translating the classic college to a contemporary form and incorporating the DNA of Jacobsen's own practice. Even in a city so steeped in British tradition, he saw no place for Gothic ornamentation or soaring rooms but aimed for a more subdued – yet distinct – architectural expression[103] in keeping with St Catherine's motto *Nova et Vetera* (the old and the new).[104]

In a speech – probably written for Prince Philip's visit to St Catherine's on 22 May 1964 – Jacobsen summed up his design strategy as follows:

A university suitable for present days (sic) needs could only be created using modern methods and materials.[105]

At the same time, he sought to preserve the old colleges' feeling of enclosure and their careful balance between inner and outer spaces. He was respectfully aware that he stood on the shoulders of the old master builders but also consciously embraced the expression of his own generation. He made this clear in an interview with *Berlingske Tidende*:

It is obviously not my purpose here to try to reform or change traditions that are centuries old and which have yielded such excellent results. – I dare say that in Oxford, we find good architecture representing all historical periods and styles from the 15th century on; all that is missing is our own time, and that is what I will attempt to represent. [...] For posterity, St Catherine's College will stand as an expression of mid-20th-century architecture.[106]

Jacobsen was fascinated by the student accommodation in Brasenose College across from the Radcliffe Camera by Powell & Moya Architect Practice, although it did not serve as direct inspiration, since it was so different from anything he might design. The buildings – which were four to five storeys high and made of glass, steel, and concrete – adapted precisely to the heights and widths of the end walls of the existing Victorian/Edwardian buildings. Another Danish architect, Johan Pedersen, also appreciated the qualities of these buildings:

[They] are the finest works of modern architecture in England. [The project is] especially beautiful, both in itself and in its adaptation to the old buildings it was so sublimely built in between, up to, and around. The solution is ingenious yet strangely convincing.[107]

North of Museum Road lies St John's College, which Jacobsen also visited, although that also did not become a model for his design of Catz. The 154 new student dwellings by Architects' Co-Partnership, which doubled the college's capacity, were among the few new ones in the city. It was the adaptation of the project to the existing setting that drew the architects' interest in their effort to find a contemporary interpretation of a college.

---

102) Bullock, A. (1984). *How St Catherine's College came to be founded* [A talk given to the Middle Common Room of St Catherine's College on 31 May 1984 by the Founding Master, Lord Bullock of Leafield; verbatim transcript] (p. 47). (LXIC Box: Talks by Lord Bullock and others: Oral history).
103) Faber, T. (1968). *Arne Jacobsen* (p. 22). Tiranti.
104) *Arne Jacobsen Buildings* (p. 15). (2010). Books LLC.

105) *St. Catherine's College Oxford*. Danish National Archives (Business Archive). Correspondence 1963, 1964 (283), p. 3.
106) Mentze, E. (1959, 19 April). Teknik og aandfuldt haandværk samles i St. Catherine's College. *Berlingske Tidende*, 18.

107) Pedersen, J. (1964). Arne Jacobsen i Oxford. *Gutenberghus Årsskrift*, 35–36. See also College Builders Meet the Demands of a Perfectionist (1964, 30 July). *Building Industry News*.

Above: Powell & Moya became known for their modernist buildings in both Oxford and Cambridge. In 1962, the Brasenose College magazine *The Brazen Nose* reported, 'Powell & Moya have made a great success of a most difficult assignment: the architectural equivalent of a century in bad light on a turning wicket. On a site which had little to commend it they have produced a building with dignity and charm which is admirably adapted to the purpose it is to serve.' The new student rooms make up staircases 16–18 and are known among the undergraduates as the 'car park' and 'the bunker'.

Below: The student accommodation at St John's College was completed between 1958 and 1960 as the first modern buildings erected in an Oxford college for more than a century. The design, created by Michael Powers of the avant-garde firm Architects' Co-Partnership (ACP), reformed the city's college architecture and were aptly named 'the Beehives'.

A stranger comes to town

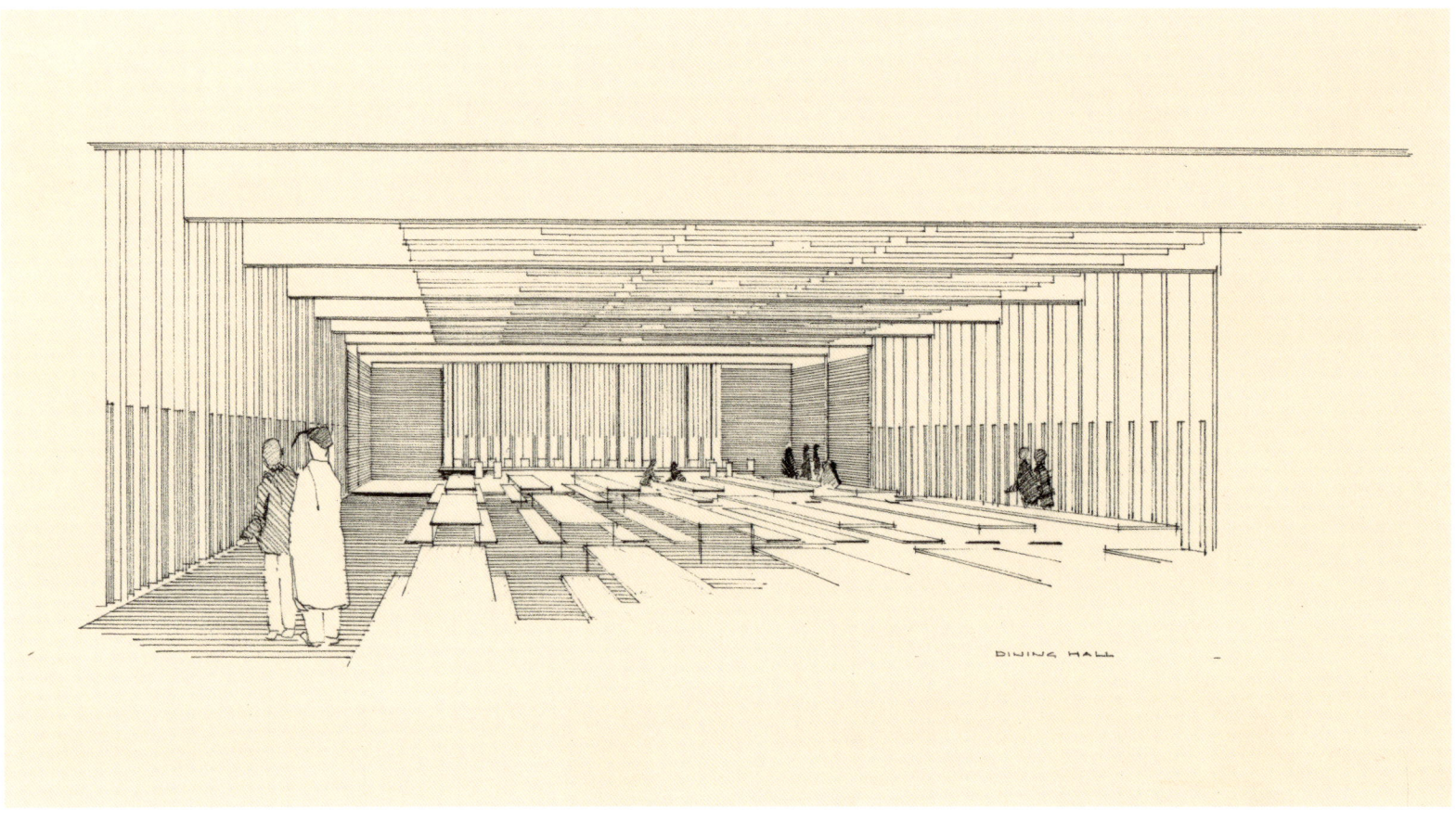

Perspective of the Dining Hall. Originally, it was not furnished with chairs but with benches.

The official openings of the new college

Catz was constructed in stages, with the work continuing as funding came through. At the official opening in 1964, *The Guardian* estimated the total costs at £2.75 million, with £2.4 million raised at that point.[108] The first dwellings, the Junior Common Room and the Middle Common Room (MCR), went into use in 1962 – the official opening took place on 16 October 1964 with a dinner for 318 guests.[109]

Esso Petroleum Company, owned by Exxon in the USA, funded the construction of the Dining Hall.[110] At the opening event in October 1964, former Prime Minister Harold Macmillan, who was chancellor of the University, showed that he had read the room with this cheeky comment addressed at the sponsors:

This Dining Hall must be the most expensive filling station they've erected for some time.[111]

Esso's board members had a roaring laugh, and four days later, they approved the plaque for the hall: 'This Hall was given to St Catherine's College by Esso Petroleum Company'.[112]

On 26 October 1966, the official opening of the Bernard Sunley Building, which contains a lecture theatre and meeting rooms, marked the conclusion of Arne Jacobsen's work in Oxford. Only the entrance to the university grounds remained outstanding.

---

108) Mr Macmillan praises a great Dane. (1964, 17 October). *The Guardian*.

109) Arne Jacobsen was not seated at High Table but at a table across from Alan Bullock's. St Catherine's College, Oxford. Official Opening, Friday, October 16th, 1964. Seating Plan.

110) Translation of a Motto. (1964–65). *Esso Magazine*, *14*(1), 13–15. (Box 9_6_More Press Cuttings).

111) Bullock, A. (1984). *How St Catherine's College came to be founded* [A talk given to the Middle Common Room of St Catherine's College on 31 May 1984 by the Founding Master, Lord Bullock of Leafield; verbatim transcript] (p. 42). (LXIC Box: Talks by Lord Bullock and others: Oral history); Léger, J.-M. (2013). *Arne Jacobsen: Le College Ste Catherine à Oxford 1959-1964*. Moniteur Architecture AMC.

112) Danish National Archives (Business Archive). Correspondence 1964, 1965 (284).

The Master's chair for High Table Dinner and the Senior Common Room was specially designed for St Catherine's and produced in red or tan leather.

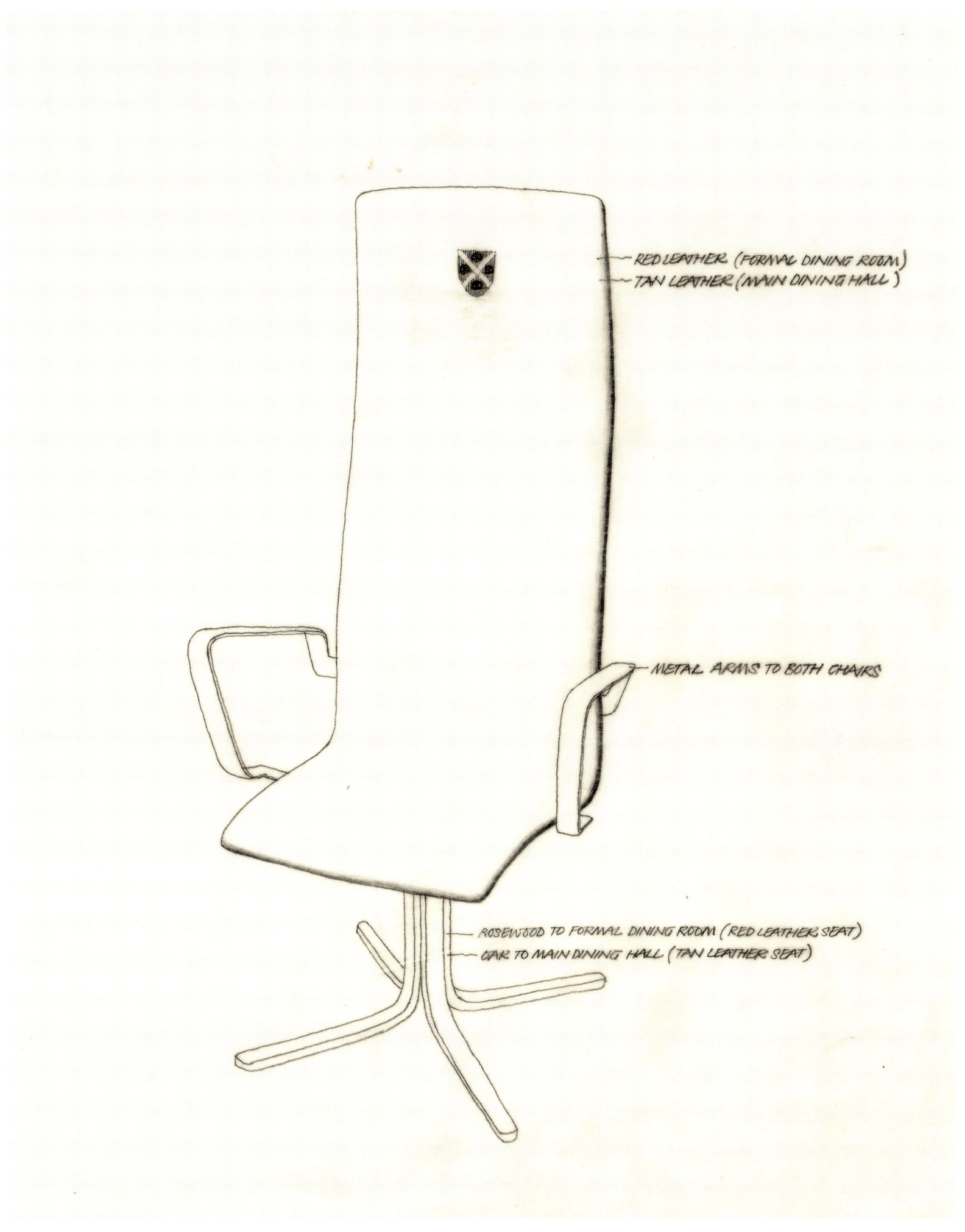

Jacobsen of and in Oxford

The brand new Catz is ready for use. The main entrance, which was relocated in connection with later expansions, was then reached via the road seen in the right section of the photo. After passing the Master's house with the walled-in private garden, you would then turn left towards the west wing. The path to the entrance first traversed the lawn, then the narrow water garden along the facade.

Danish caricaturists loved to portray Arne Jacobsen. In this drawing from 31 August 1963, Bo Bojesen illustrates the 'bed architecture problem' that had arisen when American Vice President Lyndon B. Johnson spent a night at the new SAS Hotel. Johnson was more than 6 feet 3 inches tall.

The Danish comic strip 'Esben Kvadersten, Architect' is a satirical take on the architect as the designer of total works of design – here including the chair, shoes, and table – and an affectionate comment on fancy but useless designs. The strip is not a direct caricature of Arne Jacobsen, but considering how few architects in 1959 were able to create such a Gesamtkunstwerk, it seems obvious that the cartoonist, Jørgen Mogensen, would have been inspired by the vast scope of work of Denmark's best-known architect-designer. [118]

The correspondent for *Politiken* described the new college as a stringent but 'distinctive new feature in the city'.[113] His portrayal of Jacobsen's struggle followed the format of a familiar film plot, with a protagonist facing epic challenges and struggles before finally emerging victorious, celebrated by the people. He debated whether such 'ascetic rigour' was a fit for Jacobsen's portfolio and ultimately argued that it was an apt narrative for the British university tradition. Ending on a somewhat bombastic note, he asserted that the architecture was neither Danish nor British:

> [This is] *the only valuable work of architecture in Oxford from the last two hundred years.*

Similar high praise was offered by architect Richard Sheppard, who in a private letter lauded the exquisite craftsmanship on display:

> *The standard of your detailing even recalls the Greeks.*[114]

Under the headline 'Not a Dane but Arne Jacobsen', *Politiken*'s correspondent, J. Anker Nielsen, added to the praise heaped on the architect,[115] quoting the client, Alan Bullock, who underscored that the choice of architect was based on merit, not on nationality; just as with music, Bullock listened to what he liked, nothing else. In retrospect, the British architect Adrian Friend was enthusiastic about Jacobsen's total-design approach, which was also at play in the contemporary SAS Hotel.

> *Nowadays there is a lot of talk about iconic architecture, but back then it was the ideas that made architecture iconic.*[116]

This approach represented the realisation of what remained an unattainable utopia to ordinary people, in which the brilliant architect, like a god, shaped an entire universe, from bolt to city. For St Catherine's, Jacobsen and his studio designed everything from ashtrays and door handles, colour schemes, bedspreads, curtains, carpets, furniture, and lighting to the buildings themselves and the garden plan.[117] The universal man, as Reyner Banham called this architectural creator:

> *The* uomo universale, *the man who is omnicompetent, will always demand to be omnipotent. If he can do everything in sight then by God he'll want to – among other things, just to prove that he can.*[119]

Berlingske Tidende's critic, Carsten Fälling, on the other hand, saw a fruitful fusion of the best of Danish architecture and British university history.[120] He saw this departure from the custom of having locals carry out a national project as the primary achievement in itself. As a foreigner, he had faced additional challenges of finding the right materials for the job and grasping how a project of this kind was funded by private donations, which had delayed the final stage, the construction of the lecture theatre.

In *Berlingske Aftenavis*, the project was reviewed by Anders Bodelsen, who would go on to become one of Denmark's most acclaimed and widely read novelists.[121] With a background in unfinished studies in law, literature, and economics, he worked as a freelance writer, with architecture as one of his topics. His background is evident in the language of the review, which is less technical and more evocative and academic. Thus, he wrote that the window apertures were covered by an 'enormous fishtank window', while the bricks were described as having the colour of brown Norwegian whey cheese.

At this point, we are approaching the mid-1960s. A young person himself, Bodelsen noted that the students were almost demonstratively informally dressed in this city clad in tradition. Academic accomplishments meant more, heritage less. This reflected the beginnings of the growing democratisation during this decade, which, however, was

113) Hartmann-Petersen, J. (1964, 24 July). Jacobsen of Oxford. *Politiken*, 9–10.

114) Letter from Richard Sheppard dated 26 May 1965. St. Catherine's College Oxford. Danish National Archives (Business Archive). Correspondence 1965, 1968 (285).

115) Nielsen, J.A. (1964, 24 July). Ikke en dansker, men Arne Jacobsen. *Politiken*, 10.

116) St Hill, C. (2012). It is 50 years since St Catherine's, the youngest of the Oxford University colleges, was designed by Arne Jacobsen. *Blueprint* (London, England), (318), 29.

117) Rigsarkivet (Erhvervsarkivet). Correspondence and more with Holscher 1962, 1966 (286).

118) Esben Kvadersten arkitekt M.A.A.(1959). *Arkitekten*, 61(20), 364.

119) Russell, J. (1964, 26 July). The master builder. *The Sunday Times*, 12.

120) Fälling, C. (1964, 26 July). Moderne dansk arkitektur og engelsk tradition. *Berlingske Tidende*, Sec. 2, 7.

121) Bodelsen, A. (1963, 18 July). Jacobsen i Oxford. *Berlingske Aftenavis*, 4.

The garden plan is just as significant as the building architecture, as illustrated by the empty spaces formed by parallel walls of ochre-coloured limestone from the official opening. Today, they have turned into ribbons of dense yew hedges.

Right: The Library Building with greenish-brown copper flashing. The beam pierces the glass in the tall, narrow window, giving the impression that the delicate mullions carry the weight.

still too immature for Jacobsen's architecture. The building materials – steel, bricks, and cement – expressed a strict and determined architecture that engaged in a pleasantly free relationship with the English tradition, in Bodelsen's opinion. Thus, he concluded that not only had Oxford gained a purposeful college for its money; more importantly, it had gained a work of art, a challenge, and 'a model for future projects'.

After a visit to St Catherine's on 30 June 1963, city planner Thomas Sharp was breathless with excitement. The author of *Town and Townscape*, Sharp was one of Britain's great thinkers shaping the modern urban approach to city planning, which was moving away from the Garden City movement. In a private thank-you note to Bullock, Sharp wrote,

> *I think you are getting the best buildings that Oxford has had for a hundred years and more; and among the very best in Britain in this century. So I rejoice for you – and for us all.*[122]

Bullock could not have received better feedback from an expert, who during the tour had pointed out details that Bullock himself had overlooked. In a meeting with Lankester, Jacobsen had in fact mentioned that Sharp's book *Oxford Replanned* was on his wish list.[123]

While the press and the leading architecture critics were full of praise, some saw St Catherine's ascetic repetition as dull and un-British. *The Guardian's* Diana Rowntree declared that even if tourists had invaded Alan Bullock's home, the strict order made the college unsuitable for sightseeing:

> *There is nothing picturesque about it, and the unfamiliar details, seen out of context, seem downright ugly. The siting gives nothing away.*[124]

At this early stage, while the concrete construction was still naked and bare, the buildings could in fact have been a tourist attraction, because the rhythm of the concrete framework 'must have been as impressive as the ruined Parthenon'. This unyielding order was the impressive feature. Even though the Hall, the library, and the lecture theatre clearly varied in purpose, height and character, they all had the same 11 columns, which carried identical beams. In a Beatles era, Rowntree concluded,

> *This most classical building in the least classical of cities has the Liverpool sound.*

In its satirical section, *Berlingske Aftenavis* fused St Catherine's with the SAS building (home to the SAS Royal Hotel) in Copenhagen, skewering both projects under the motto 'Better to get it wrong than to get nothing at all!'

> *As a curious fact, we can share that Arne Jacobsen for his college in Oxford used virtually the same drawings that he used for the Royal Hotel, except that the tall building was here laid on its side, so that people are walking on the walls, not on the floor, which instead is papered.*[125]

122) The Garden City movement was an urban planning movement in the early 20th century that promoted satellite communities placed around the central city, separated by greenbelts. These garden cities contained residential areas, industry and farms. (XL Box 10. The Founding Master).

123) IIJ Box 1_The Architect-appointment-note by Lord Bullock – correspondence: 4_Correspondence on choice of architect, 1959.
124) Rowntree, D. (1964, 24 July). Ordered Simplicity. *The Guardian*.

125) *Berlingske Aftenavis*. Found in Arne Jacobsen's personal scrapbooks.

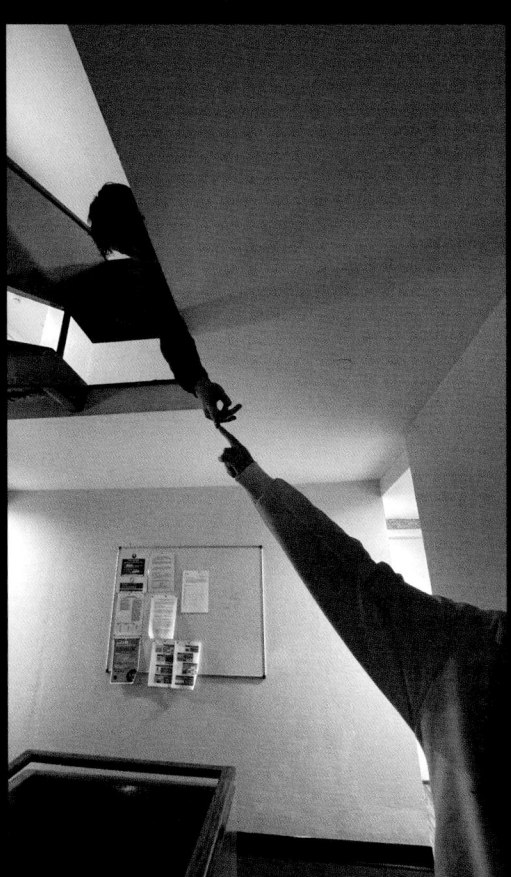

Catz is like a Danish person

Martin Alfonsin Larsen, Music

As noted by Martin Alfonsin Larsen, there is something very Danish about the 'reserved' Catz. However, once you get to know the place, 'there's a world there'. Like this rainbow above the library, which is also open to interpretation.

❛ A bit intimidating, but also quite beautiful.

What were your first impressions when you first arrived at St Catherine's?

I came in March of 2022 for the first time, so that would have been after receiving my offer two months earlier. And I thought it was a bit intimidating with the big buildings, which can feel quite hulking. But in a lot of ways, I also thought it was very beautiful, because it was springtime, so it was quite warm. I'd say the greenery in Catz is definitely very beautiful. I was speaking to some people on a telephone campaign a couple of weeks ago who had said, 'Oh, it was completely not beautiful when we were here'. And I think that's a highlight of it; there's a lot of greenery in the space. So maybe the tagline of that would be 'a bit intimidating, but also quite beautiful'.

How does the architecture, design, or landscape affect you in your everyday life?

I stay in Catz a lot, especially because my faculty is 25 minutes away. So it often feels like running a marathon, walking to get to Christ Church, which is where the Music Faculty is. There are things I really like about Catz; I think the Dining Hall is lovely. The JCR and the Dining Halls are very social spaces, and I've made a lot of friends in them. There are friends that I've made where we just see each other at lunch or dinner, and we come and sit together. I will say that I'm not the biggest fan of the lamps on the dining tables, especially because if there's a big conversation that's going on, or if there's a big dinner, it can definitely block your view of people. That is sometimes a bit frustrating. But it's a relatively minor grievance.

And I really love my room. I don't like having to move out at the end of every term, and the single beds are also quite small. But the architecture affects me a lot, because I'm here so much, by virtue of not leaving the college as much as maybe other people do. But no, I think it's very enjoyable to be in. I don't have any poignant words to put in to explain why it affects me so much. I think it's a lovely space to be in, despite, you know, some of the problems that it might have.

Is there a room, place, or section that is your favourite – or least favourite – location, and why?

I think that for me, it's the Dining Hall. Again, because I've made so many friends just by virtue of being there. And in a lot of ways, it feels like a traditional Oxford dining hall but inverted and very grand. That's what I think more generally about this college. I think it's incredible, because you have the quad in the middle; you've got the rooms; you've got the Dining Hall; but it feels distinctly modern with the furniture and architecture. I come to the Dining Hall for almost every meal, so that's my favourite place.

If you had to use a metaphor for St Catherine's character, what would it be?

This might sound a bit silly at first, but it feels like a Danish person. I come from a family of Danes, and they can be a bit reserved at first, with how they speak to you and how they treat you. Even with my family, I feel that way sometimes. There's definitely an aspect of distance, but when you get them to open up, there's a world there, and they're very sweet, very empathetic, and very supportive.

I would say that Catz feels a lot like that, because when I moved in, it was a cold autumn and winter, and the buildings also felt quite cold. But you discover the Dining Hall, you discover the JCR, you make friends, and things change. You change the way your room looks to feel more adapted to you.

The character is a big part of why I applied here. I had heard about the history, and I had seen the college on Google. I had never come to Oxford before I'd been accepted, but there was definitely a feeling that I thought this would be a cool place to be, especially because I thought there was some sort of Danish heritage going on there.

And that's the other thing: how many students would have gone through these rooms now? I mean, there must have been at least 50 students staying in my room, and that's when you're not even thinking about the people that have stayed there for conferences or those people who have probably made the room their own. You get a real chance to do that when you stay here for longer than two months. I mean, obviously it's an annoyance to pack all your stuff up. But you know, getting to stay here for effectively six months a year, it's incredible. You really get to know the space.

Can you describe an instance prompted by the physical setting, architecture, or environment of Catz that was particularly memorable to you?

I have a couple, but I'll go with the nice one first. This was yesterday. I had left the room in the morning, and the sun still wasn't out properly. And then I came back at around 4 pm, after I'd finished my Collections and decided to go for a run. I quickly came in and grabbed some clothes and left, and I didn't really get time to let it soak in. But when I got back, I just noticed that the sun was shining through the windows. And that's something that I hadn't seen in months, because it was always cold and dark, or when the sun was out, I'd be outside or walking back from faculty. And it was very strange, because it's this very normal thing, but I'd never experienced it in that space before.

The second instance was prompted by the gym building. There's so much totality of vision in Catz; it feels a lot like one person built it, in a sense. I've heard this story, but I've never checked if it's true. I heard that Arne Jacobsen was going through a divorce when he designed Catz, so that's why he made the bed single. And I thought, 'That's probably not true', but I thought it was quite funny. And then he did his six days of creation, and on the seventh day, he said, 'Oh, damn, I can't be bothered. I'm just gonna stick the box there'. Jacobsen didn't design it, but it is funny to me that you have this amazing modern college. Obviously, a lot of people are very critical of the architecture; people have many thoughts about it, especially if they're from an old college, like Christ Church, or Balliol, or Trinity, or any college like that. But you have this incredible quad with these amazing buildings, this amazing accommodation. You can have your opinions... and then you have the gym building in the corner.

Is there anything we haven't talked about that you would like to cover?

Well, I would just like to say that I think that Catz has one of the most social communities. And I think that is kind of fostered by the architecture. Especially in the JCR – we have one of the biggest JCRs in Oxford, and the drinks are cheap. The Dining Hall is huge; the food is also very cheap. So I think that does actually facilitate people hanging out and there being a sense of a very social community.

The kitchen and the bathroom are the two frustrating parts of my experience. At Catz, the only thing that I find difficult is that there's one kitchen for a floor of about 12 people. The bathroom is the same; there's one toilet for six people in my part of the staircase, and there's one toilet for the rest on the other side, and there are two showers. Those private spaces... 'frustrating' is the word I would use to describe them. Especially if you have more than two people in the kitchen. It's like playing musical chairs. You know, you have to grate past each other to get to the relevant places; it can be frustrating in that sense.

IV

Lovelace College

In the world of film, architecture is an ever-present character. It is the set that frames the plot, and it plays an active role by defining the space. The word 'plot' is key in both architecture and film. To an architect, a plot is a site, a delineated space; in film, it is a sequence of events that play out over a limited period of time.

The events in a plot 'take place', and Oxford is an excellent setting for films. With its tall towers, pointy spires, open courtyards, narrow lanes, overgrown facades, and long arcades, Oxford is an incredibly cinematic city. Sherlock Holmes, Laurel & Hardy, and Harry Potter are just some of the famous film and TV characters who have visited the city. *Oxford Blues* (1984) and *The Oxford Murders* (2008) are naturally also set here. In box-office hits such as *A Fish Called Wanda* (1988), *Howards End* (1992), and *Saving Private Ryan* (1998), parts of the plot play out in these Gothic surroundings. That is the attraction – the old, Gothic Oxford.

Nevertheless, St Catherine's College, too, has found its way, if not to the silver screen, then to the TV screen. In 2017, St Catherine's College was the setting of an episode in one of ITV's biggest hits in the detective genre, *Endeavour*, which deals with the early years of charismatic detective Endeavour Morse and his personal and professional trials and tribulations.

In 'Game', the first episode of Season 4 in the series, St Catherine's College appears under the fictitious name Lovelace College. The inspiration for this name is not explained, but since the plot revolves around the development of artificial intelligence, it is likely that it refers to Augusta Ada King (1815–1852), Countess of Lovelace, who is regarded as the world's first programmer.[126] Ada King recognised that the 'analytical engine', the computer, had potential applications that went beyond mere calculations, and her notes outline the contours of the software that, as 'a collaborative tool', was capable of both crunching numbers and creating art (specifically music).[127] She referred to her work as 'poetical science'.[128]

On 8 January 2017, 'Game' premiered on British TV. 'Poetical science' is the dominant theme of the episode. The Gothic skyline of historic Oxford, usually seen in the golden light of the setting sun, is a sort of signature for *Endeavour* as well as for the earlier series *Inspector Morse*, which deals with Morse's later years.[129] The city below is the setting of the dark cases that Morse is charged with solving. What stands out about the episode featuring 'Lovelace College' is that it is not set in the dark, gloomy city with its strange figures and mysterious traditions but in an ultramodern college, whose windows signal light, clarity, and transparency. The episode is shot in dark, dusty, brownish shades, pointing back to the old Oxford, but the plot deals with perhaps the most modern theme of all: our relationship with modern technology. Scholars at 'Lovelace' are working to develop a computer that is so advanced that it can challenge the Russian computer scientist Yuri Gradenko to a game of chess. Man against machine.

With its straight lines and right angles informed by the modern machine aesthetic that was propagated, especially, by Le Corbusier, Arne Jacobsen's college forms the perfect setting of this show-down. The Danish connection is suggested through the presence of a scientist with the Danish-sounding name Richard Nielsen, who is involved in the development of the computer, called Joint Computing Nexus (J-C-N) or 'Jason', as the British opponent to the Russian Gradenko.

When Nielsen is found drowned in a river under a bridge, his death is initially believed to be either suicide or accidental. Soon, however, two more bodies are found in the public pool, Cowley Baths, and when a fourth body appears, DC Morse suspects a pattern.

On his first visit to 'Lovelace College', Morse goes to Dr Nielsen's office on the ground floor. The window panes show the reflections of pink blossoms on the trees – and of the person who followed him there. Morse flips through a stack of books, the top one being *Chess Lessons for Beginners*. On the wall is a picture of salmon flies.

On his next visit, Morse is introduced to Yuri Gradenko in the Senior Common Room. In the park, there is a giant chess set. The Russian addresses Morse in his native language, and Morse impresses him by replying in Russian.

---

126) Remarkably, in the Wikipedia article about Ada Lovelace's appearance as a character in popular culture from her birth until now, 'Lovelace College' and *Endeavour* are not included. See https://en.wikipedia.org/wiki/Ada_Lovelace (last accessed 21 November 2022).

127) https://en.wikipedia.org/wiki/Ada_Lovelace#cite_note-ABCL-6 (last accessed 19 November 2022).

128) In 2009, Britain introduced an annual Ada Lovelace Day aiming to 'raise the profile of women in science, technology, engineering, and maths' and to 'create new role models for girls and women' in these fields. (Ibid.)

129) The award-winning series *Inspector Morse* (portrayed by John Thaw) and his assistant Sergeant Lewis (portrayed by Kevin Whately) is a 33-episode series originally shown between 6 January 1987 and 15 November 2000 on Central Independent Television (ITV). In the final episode, 'The Remorseful Day', DCI Morse dies from heart failure due to excessive alcohol consumption.
Any notion of resuming the series with John Thaw as the lead was impossible, as Thaw himself passed away in 2002. Due to the series' popularity – in 2018, the readers of TV magazine *Radio Times* selected it as the best British detective series ever – it was followed up by the series *Inspector Lewis*, originally aired from 29 January 2006 to 10 November 2015, also on ITV. The latest spinoff of *Inspector Morse* is *Endeavour* with Shaun Evans as Morse.

Morse in front of his 1960 Jaguar Mark 2, 2.4L, with 'Lovelace College' in the background. In 'Game', St Catherine's College is the setting of the unfolding plat, just as several of Oxford's other historic buildings and crooked streets have been since the initial series, Inspector Morse, was launched in 1987.

Below: Morse in a conversation with Yuri Gradenko next to the rectangular water garden with the terraces running the full length of the site on the west side of 'Lovelace College'. Other Oxford colleges have also appeared in the series under fictitious names, including Alfreda's College (Trinity), Baidley College (Keble), Hescott College (Oriel), and Lonsdale College (Brasenose), to mention just a few.

Bottom: Jason's victory over Yuri Gradenko is celebrated with champagne in the Quad in 'Lovelace College'.

Jason outperforms the human brain. The Brits celebrate the victory on the lawn in the centre of 'Lovelace College', while Morse questions the beautiful Dr Pat Amory under the loggia, the open walkway running along the sides of the college building. She insists that she and Dr Nielsen were just friends and did not have a romantic relationship. Morse sees Yuri Gradenko standing on the other side of the building towards the lake and the pink-blossomed trees. The Russian tells Morse about his close friendship with Dr Nielsen and reveals that they had engaged in an extensive correspondence about chess but especially about the 'threat to the world posed by the ideologies of our respective governments'. He also reveals that Dr Nielsen's team was internally conflicted.

After Gradenko and his bodyguards have left, Morse spots another scholar in the opposite arcade, Dr Carson, who refuses to provide access to confidential information due to his low position in the hierarchy. Finally, journalist Tessa Knight intercepts Morse to exchange information off the record, but the following day, the front page of the *Oxford Mail* reads, 'Three Drownings – Police say "Murder"'. This blatant violation of the unwritten rules of the relationship causes anger and consternation throughout the police department. Morse crosses over towards the 'Lovelace College' car park and gets into his iconic 1960 Jaguar Mark 2, 2.4L.

Lovelace College

The intention of architecture in 'Game'

Morse in the deceased Dr Nielsen's office with the ambiguous reflections in the window pane. St Catherine's College not only served as the setting of Endeavour but also of 'Terra Nullius' in the Netflix series The Crown. Catz appears as a hotel and dining hall in Tasmania in Season 4, Episode 6, which deals with Princess Diana and Prince Charles's stormy marriage.

The most recent film to be shot at Catz is *Club Zero* (2023) by director Jessica Hausner, a dark comedy about absent parents, brainwashing, and eating disorders. The film takes place at a private school (Catz) and tells the story of five students who, for individual reasons, sign up for the school's 'Conscious Eating' course. The course is about eating less and less to achieve greater physical and mental health. The film also has a Danish connection, as the School Principal is portrayed by Sidse Babett Knudsen.

Every story has a beginning, a middle, and an end.[130] The plot unfolds over time and lends meaning to this time period. It provides a sort of understanding and explanation of the events that play out over time. However, events are things that 'take place', and thus, the plot also involves the space in which these events unfold – the site, including, in a detective story, the scene of the crime.

Our recollection of events is situated, rooted in the site where they took place. In 'Game', the architecture helps bring meaning to the sequence of events. The modern era is present in the form of modern architecture. It represents the blind faith in new technology that was common during the 1960s. Any of Oxford's older colleges could also have served as the setting of 'Game', as they contain the same basic architectural functions as St Catherine's – arcades, a central garden, data collections, lecture theatres – but due to their age, they are rooted in either the Age of Enlightenment, with its emphasis in reason and nature, or in the 19th century's 'obsession with questions of origin, evolution, progress, genealogy, its foregrounding of the historical narrative as par excellence the necessary mode of explanation and understanding', as Peter Brooks has described this century. He goes on to add, 'We know that with the advent of Modernism came an era of suspicion toward plot, engendered perhaps by an overelaboration of and overdependence on plots in the nineteenth century.'[131] Oxford changes very little, so a new college is in itself a revolution.

The intention of using St Catherine's as the set is to look to the future. This is where we should seek the answers to today's problems. In the past, we understood ourselves; in the future, we need to understand artificial intelligence. 'Game' takes place in 1967 in the most modern college in Oxford. Two years later, Neil Armstrong leaps down onto the surface of the moon from Apollo 11. An important first in human history. And without giving away the plot of 'Game', the murderer eventually breaks down in tears and explains the motive behind their actions: having faced losses in the past, the perpetrator cannot face also losing to the future, embodied by Jason, the computer that, as a quintessential representation of 'poetical science', is capable of both embracing the beauty of chess and crunching the mathematical calculations behind the game.

130) A plot has an inner 'logic', and when it is broken, this rupture either enhances or hinders our understanding, perhaps especially in fiction. Fiction can be understood in a variety of ways across different periods, but in this case, it represents 'a system of internal energies and tensions, compulsions, resistances, and desires'. Brooks, P. (1984). *Reading for the plot: Design and intention in narrative* (pp. 6, 12, 42). Alfred A. Knopf.

131) Ibid., pp. 6–7, 49.

Matriculation Day. The arcades under the student rooms keep people dry in the notoriously damp British weather.

Catz moments / Flynn Hallman, student of English

Living someone else's life

Kelsey Moriarty, History

6
Reputation as the cooler younger sibling.

Dressed in a classic evening gown, on her way to one of the parties that Oxford colleges are famous for.

Living someone else's life

What were your first impressions when you first arrived at St Catherine's?

I arrived here for the first time twice! There was one time after I had applied and got the university offer, but I didn't know if I was going to get in. I went to visit just to see what it was like. The second time I actually went was when I was moving in – I was very aware that I would have to spend a lot of time there, so I was trying to like it. I really wanted to, but I didn't feel properly like it was going to be like home. It just felt very sort of remote. It didn't feel massively like a place where one could live, be comfortable and exist properly for three years.

How does the architecture, design, or landscape affect you in your everyday life?

You're just very, very aware that you're living in a very heavily curated space. There aren't many considerations for comfort. It tends to feel like it's functionality over comfort. The cupboard space where you put your things is very small, so you feel encouraged to not have that many things. It makes me feel a lot more invested in the cult of Arne Jacobsen. Also, the bed is awful. The chairs everywhere actually are just horrible. They're not comfortable at all. They're very pretty to look at, of course, but they're not comfortable, and I'm quite worried about back problems. Also, when I come into my room, there's a step. It's sort of raised, so I trip over it almost every time. To put it all together, everything about St Catz affects the way that I live and the way that I exist day to day. I feel like everyone here is very aware of that.

Especially at the start, it felt like I was living in someone else's room and in someone else's life. And in something that Arne Jacobsen had already decided for me. He's like a god among students here, and it's mostly just a running joke, but it definitely feels like there is an overarching presence, encouraging certain ways of living and ways of existing and different practices. So it still affects me in my everyday life. I've learned to put more of myself into it and decorate it more consciously within the restraints. But there's still an overarching feeling that Arne is watching.

Is there a room, place, or section that is your favourite – or least favourite – location, and why?

My room is in staircase 13. And I don't know if you've ever walked past the bike shed and gone under the little arch. Above that, because there isn't a downstairs, there's a bridge between staircases. It's sort of a big, empty room that has a bench in it and a few old discarded signs. And it's become a really lovely social space. I feel like that was sort of accidental. I don't think it was meant to be like that. But it's just a really, really nice social space. You can go there almost any time of the day, and there's probably someone there with a cup of tea, you can sit down and have a chat, and it's lovely. It's just nice to know that there are other people who also don't want to be in their room sometimes. And obviously, before parties and things, as always, lots of noise and excitement, and it's very nice. I really like that room.

If you had to use a metaphor for St Catherine's character, what would it be?

Catz has a very constant character, which is strange because it's very much defined by the people who live in it as well as the architecture. I feel like that's something you don't get with the older colleges. You don't get that awareness of who created the building and why they created it, if they were going through a divorce, or they'd just been.

Catz exists in lots of different contexts – it's shut off and it's welcoming, it's social and it's isolating. And it's just so many opposites, all in one go, that it's so difficult to pin it down or give a metaphor. Because there's that symbiosis of people and buildings, rather than in an older college where it might just be people. At Catz, the buildings have such physical importance, as do the people within them. I suppose my thoughts on Catz are very contradictory, but living somewhere means your thoughts on it are hardly going to be simple.

Can you describe an instance prompted by the physical setting, architecture, or environment of Catz that was particularly memorable to you?

There are a lot. I mean, tripping into my room every night is one of them. Because of that raised step that I trip over every single time, without fail. Lots of these [memorable instances] are injury-related, actually! There was the time I fell down the stairs in the Library because I was wearing a really long skirt. And the time that there was an ambulance sent for me, and the paramedic took me to the upstairs bit of the porter's lodge to examine me and then couldn't because there were so many windows. All of them are quite bad actually, now that I'm thinking about it. But there are good, non-injury-related times as well. The conversation pit [in the Junior Common Room] is really good. I mean, I feel like that's something prompted by the physical setting. There are some really lovely nights, when friends from other colleges come to the Catz bar and they just sort of marvel at the bar. The Catz bar is famous – it's got its own culture.

Is there anything we haven't talked about that you would like to cover?

I feel like the culture at Catz is a very difficult thing to pin down. Arne Jacobsen is a very big deal among the students here, there are lots of rumours about his life that just sort of float around the student body. Like the thing I was telling you earlier, about Arne Jacobsen going through a divorce and choosing to make everything so uncomfortable, and that's why the beds are tiny, and the chairs are awful. That was apparently because Jacobsen was going through a divorce, or he had just been through one, and he wanted everyone to feel his pain.

But the culture of Catz, if you look at the buildings individually with the wider context of the university and the old buildings that are massively popular, it's striking how different Catz is and how differently it's treated. In the wider canon of colleges at the university, it's so different. There are stereotypes assigned to each, but the one about Catz is young, vibrant, and new. To people who go to older colleges, Catz is a disgusting new building!

I also want to mention the JCR and the people in it. The JCR committee is lovely. It's all these people who are very keen on keeping Arne Jacobsen's artistic vision and his legacy alive as well as fostering our reputation as the cooler younger sibling.

V

St Catherine's layout

ORDNANCE SURVEY
Scale: 1:2500 or 25.344 inches to 1 Mile

PLAN SP 5206

Edition of 1958

In the present context, it seems appropriate to give the floor to the architect and his staff, and advisors.

Signature drawing. Hand-drawn sketch by Arne Jacobsen that was drawn live on camera in Ole Dreyer's film Arne Jacobsen in Oxford *(1970). Uncomfortable with being the focus of attention, Jacobsen always prepared carefully. Thus, under the sketch paper, we can glimpse a map from the Ordnance Survey, scale 1:2,500, that he used as support as he explained how an intelligent idea materialised as a college.*

The description of the plans for St Catherine was published in *Official Architecture and Planning* in September 1964.[132] The authors of the article were Arne Jacobsen and his project architect Knud Holscher, the consulting engineers for construction, installations, and mechanical components, surveyors, turnkey contractors, acoustics consultants, and others. In the present context, it seems appropriate to give the floor to the architect and his staff and advisors.

They can offer readers a brief and precise introduction to the intentions behind St Catherine's plan composition, materials, construction, landscaping, and, finally, costs. To avoid repeating the description of events leading up to the construction phase, this section is left out, as it has been discussed elsewhere. Afterwards, I will add some comments to contribute further to the understanding of the layout.

132) Jacobsen, A., Holscher, K., Arup, O., Balslev, M., Northcroft, Neighbour & Nicholson, Lankester, J., Lockton, P. J., Steensen Varming Mulcahy, Petersen, J., & Marshall-Andrew and Company Limited (1964). St Catherine's College, Oxford. *Official Architecture and Planning, 27*(9), 1067, 1069, 1071. See also Skriver, P. E. (1961). St. Catherine's College, Oxford. *Arkitekten*, (1), 3–7.

St Catherine's layout

THE ARCHITECTURE AND LANDSCAPE, IN THE ARCHITECTS' OWN WORDS

St Catherine's College, Oxford

Very beautiful and clear situation plan from autumn 1960.

Next spread:

The Quad with the Library in the foreground and the accommodation blocks in the background.

St Catherine's is situated in meadowland on the east side of the historic centre of the University within a network of branches of the River Cherwell. The site is approximately rectangular, measuring an average of 800 by 400 feet, with its main axis running due north to south. As the college is some distance from the older foundations it was not thought necessary that it should be designed to blend with the existing colleges.

From the outset it was decided that it was most important for the buildings to sit within the landscape rather than to dominate it in height or massing. The main grouping is set back from the river with no block rising above the line of the surrounding trees. This permitted a maximum height of thirty feet, or three storeys, which,
with the accommodation required in relation to the size of the site, determined a comparatively built-up plan.

It was further decided that for reasons of planning and structural simplicity it would be desirable to allocate separate buildings to each of the main functions, and from this broad framework developed the conception of the college as a series of independent blocks, linked where necessary by covered ways, with paved courts and garden areas between them.

A strictly defined rectangular layout, symmetrical about its north-south axis, was decided upon for the main college complex in order to give strong visual coherence to the very diverse range of
buildings to be provided. The garden areas of various sizes between the buildings are intended as a contrast to the strict geometry and sheer surfaces of the buildings. Buildings and gardens are seen as interdependent elements, the importance of which will only emerge as the planting matures.

Along the north-south axis are placed the three main communal blocks – the Dining Hall at the north, the Library in the centre, and the auditorium block at the south. Parallel with this axis, on either side of the communal blocks, are the long three-storey residential blocks, with the fellows' sets on the ground floor and the students' bed-sitting rooms above. The common room block runs along the north end of the site, and is linked with the Dining Hall. The space bounded by the end

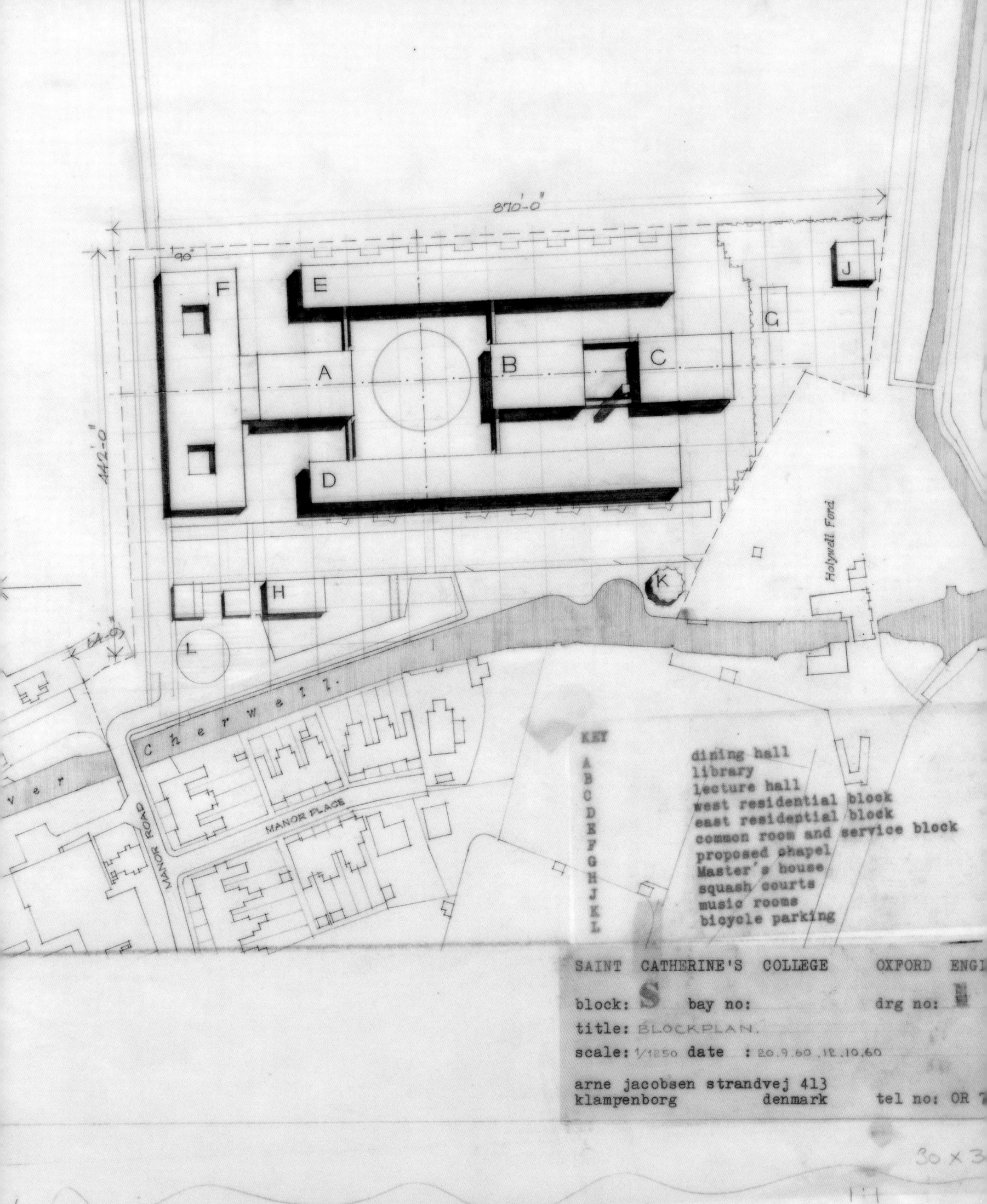

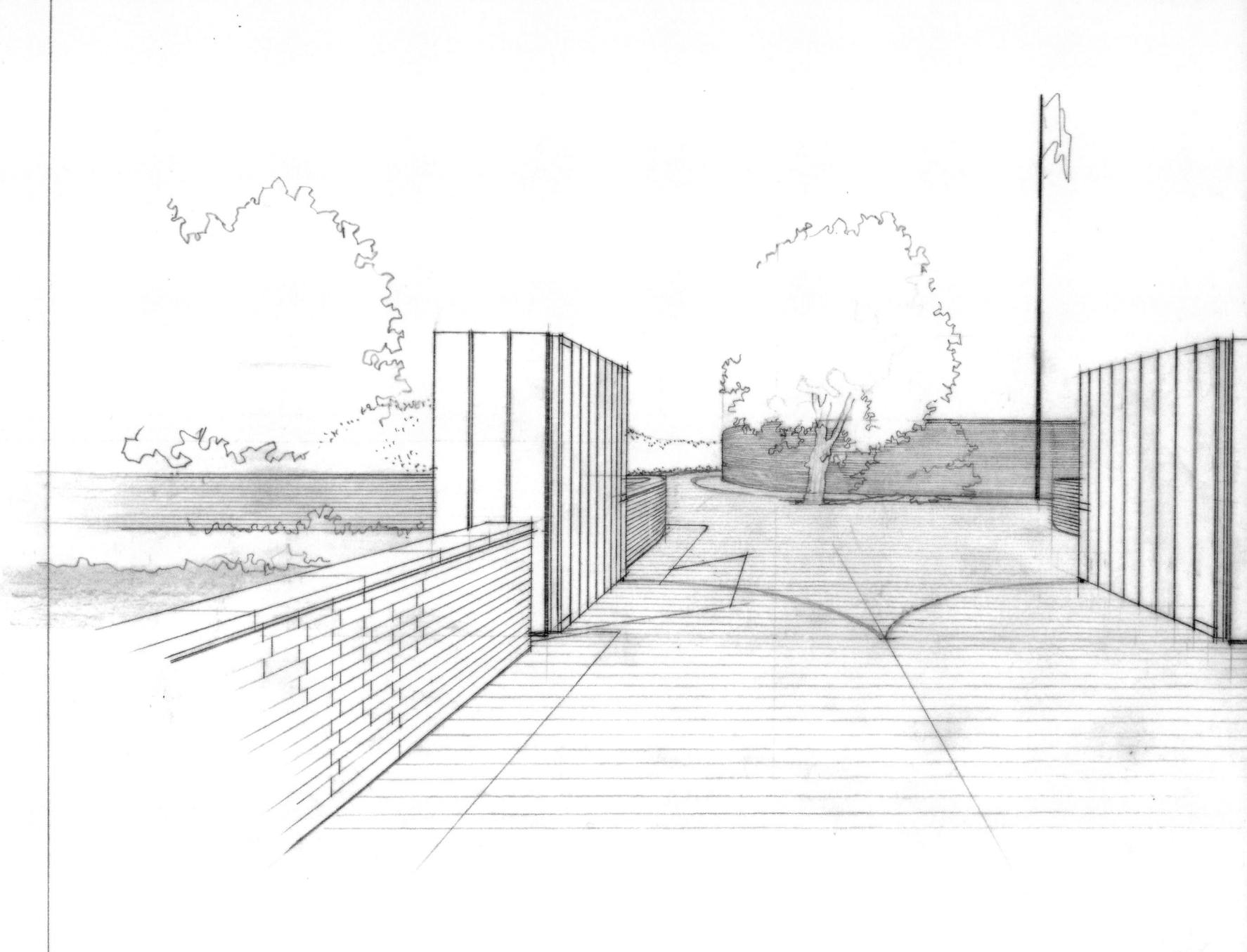

of the Dining Hall on the north, the end of the Library on the south, and the residential blocks on east and west, form the main quadrangle. The bell-tower is intended to serve as a foil to the predominantly horizontal composition of the group.

The structure of the single-storey common room block is of precast prestressed concrete beams at 8-foot centres bearing on padstones which rest on load-bearing brickwork. The residential blocks are of precast reinforced concrete frames at 10 feet 6 inches centres with insitu reinforced concrete floor slabs.

The hall, Library and auditorium blocks share a common basic structural system of precast reinforced concrete cruciform columns at 10 feet 6 inches centres carrying prestressed main beams 5 feet deep, 6 inches wide and 79 feet long with a tree span of 56 feet supporting secondary beams at 8-foot centres. This structure is enclosed in different ways in the three blocks according to the different functions performed by each building. Special 2-inch yellow bricks have been used throughout. The beams and columns generally are of smooth precast reinforced concrete. Internally the walls are generally of fair-faced brick, with painted hessian on block walls and panelling in some public rooms. Except in the hall, Library and auditorium, where they are bronze, windows and fascias are painted aluminium. Finishes throughout are of an exceptionally high standard; this is particularly true of the concrete beams and columns.

The approximate cost of the college, excluding the cost of piling, fittings and loose furniture, was £1,293,000 [converted to 2024 figures, this is the equivalent of £32.8 million].[133]

---

133) in2013dollars.com/uk/inflation/1964?amount=1293000 (calculated 13 April 2024).

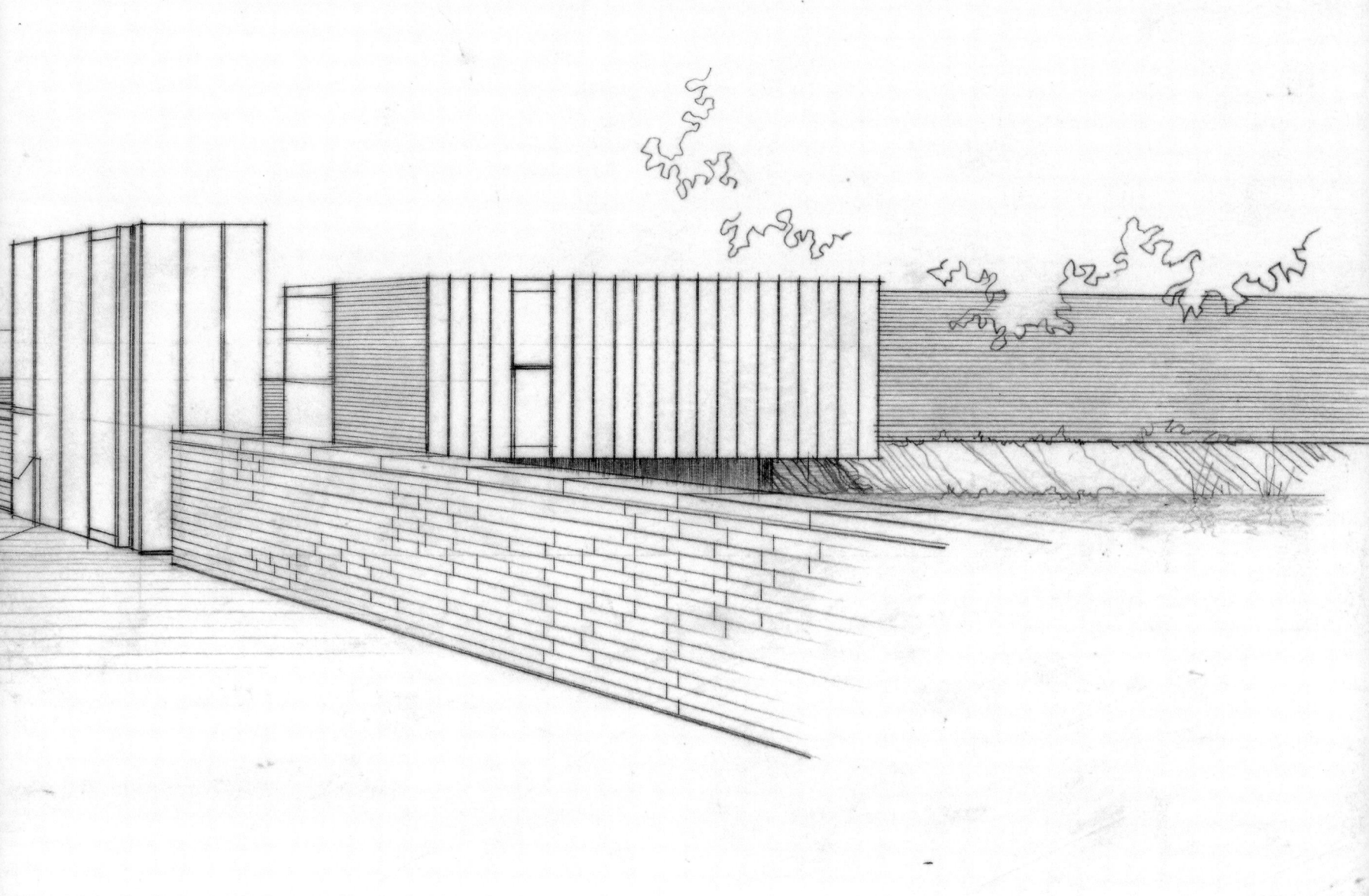

Perspective of the main entrance. The drawing shows an early – never built – perspective of the main entrance with gates on the entrance bridge, a small, adjoining structure for the Porter's Lodge, and the circular bicycle shed in the background.

Next spread:

The Quad with 300 new students on their way to have the 'freshers' group photo taken. Again, we see how appropriate the buildings are as a setting of instruction.

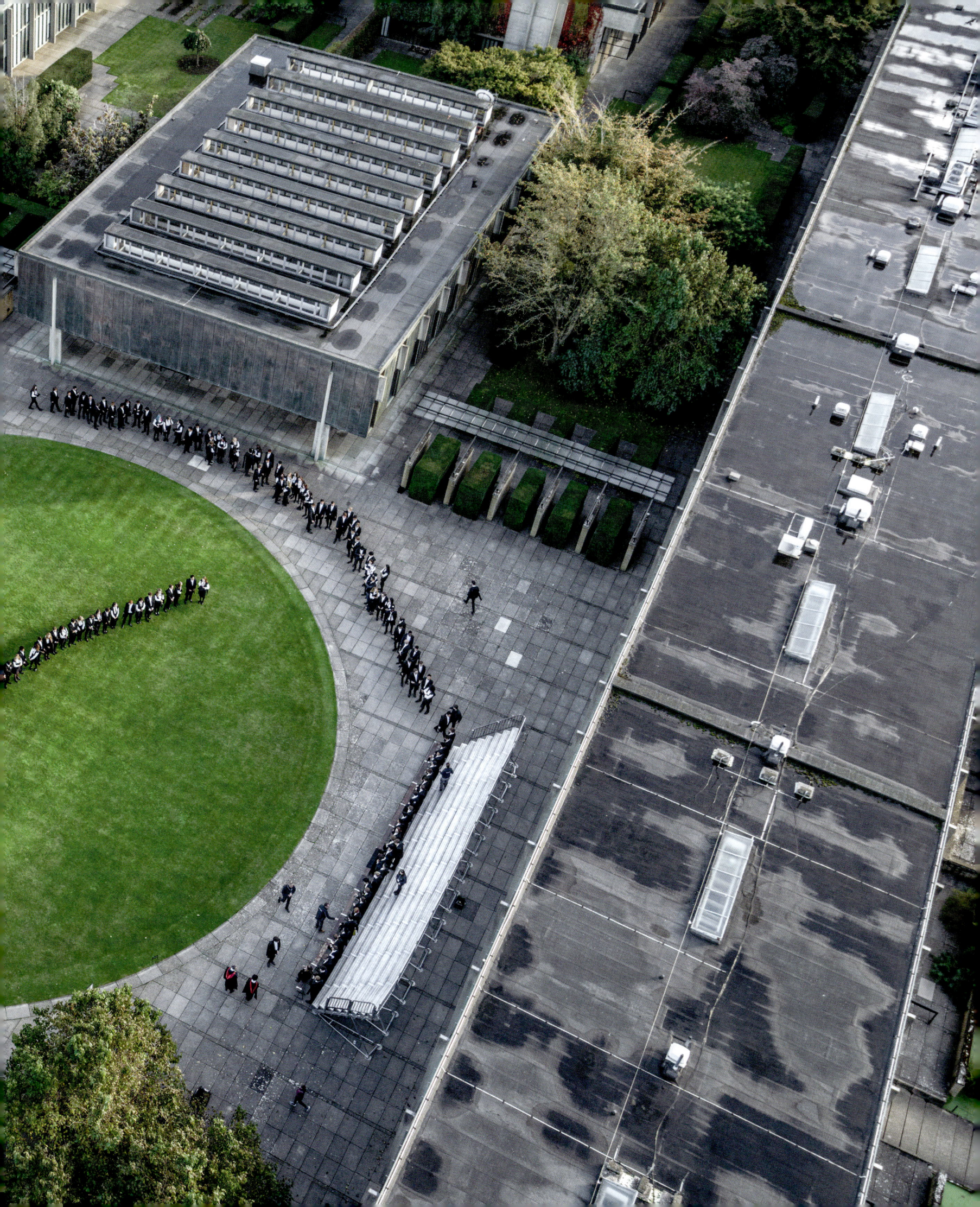

> St Catherine's is a town with many entrances, fords, and inner corridors with individuals occupying their own little worlds. [...] It is a complex town, both in its physical layout and in the hearts of those who inhabit it.

A town with many entrances

An intersection in the middle: in the bottom of the photo, the sports pavilion at Merton College; on the left, St Catherine's College as Arne Jacobsen left it; on the right, expansions by Hodder Associates, and Purcell (not visible in the photo); and in the background, the historic Oxford. The photo illustrates the beautiful simplicity of the plan from the official opening in 1964 to the present day. See map on page 12.

Next spread:

With its classic symmetry, the college was, from the outset, conceived as a complete design, rather than as a cellular structure that would allow future extensions.

St Catherine's College has a simple layout, but the experience is complex. As the American sociologist Joseph A. Soares observed, Oxford colleges were a paradox: they were private, enclosed, communal places that had all the best qualities of public space.[134]

The main complex consists simply of six rectangular buildings distributed along a symmetrical axis and a circular central quadrangle, which is a significant element of Oxford colleges.

The original source of this situational typology is the monastery. Surrounded by thick walls, it provided light, a sense of security, and a rational organisation. Outside, chaos, danger, and nature reigned; inside, 'cosmic order, complete worlds in miniature'.[135] Thus, St Catherine's possesses two fundamental Oxford elements: a common public square and a staircase system. The Quadrangle at Catz pulls the buildings together, while the system of student rooms arranged around a staircase provides an intimate feel:

> [A] *relation between city and landscape as equally valuable components of the metropolitan landscape can be created.*[136]

The emphasis is on a calm horizontal structure, with no building exceeding three storeys in height, except for the bell tower. The risk that this perfectionist architectural style has to avoid is neither pretentiousness nor the self-absorption that sometimes characterises modern British academia, but boredom.[137] However, St Catherine's is anything but boring.

Reyner Banham, the author of *Los Angeles: The Architecture of Four Ecologies* (1971), a groundbreaking book on modern architecture in the United States, was aware of the risk of boredom but concluded that Arne Jacobsen had succeeded in creating an interesting interplay between Catz's constituent parts:

> *In spite of the visual, functional and psychological isolation of block from block, the assembly of objects on this ideal surface holds together as an immutable architectural unity.*[138]

Only the Music House, the Master's house, the bell tower, and the bike shed fall outside the grid. It is easy to get lost at Catz. Although there is a single centre, the Quad, this space does not provide an easy overview or insight. St Catherine's is a town with many entrances, fords, and inner corridors with individuals occupying their own little worlds. There are boulevards leading to the centre but also plenty of side streets to lose oneself in. It is a complex town, both in its physical layout and in the hearts of those who inhabit it. The different parts of the town, each one an aesthetic accomplishment in its own right, offers a sense of cohesion but not without an active effort from its citizens.

> *At St. Catherine's, the ideal plane surface of the paving makes a kind of ideal, random, democratic circulation possible throughout the spaces between the buildings.*[139]

---

134) Soares, J. A. (1999). *The Decline of Privilege: The Modernization of Oxford University* (p. 136). Stanford University Press.
135) de Wit, S. (2018). *Hidden Landscapes: The metropolitan garden as a multi-sensory expression of place* (p. 156). Architectura & Natura.
136) Ibid., p. 357.
137) Sådan siger de andre. (1961). *Arkitekten, 63*(1), A 26, A 28; Dansk arkitekt bedømt i England. (1961, 18 January). *Demokraten*, 4.
138) Banham, R. (1964). Criticism: St Catherine's College, Oxford, Churchill College, Cambridge. *The Architectural Review, 136* (811), 176.
139) Ibid., p. 177.

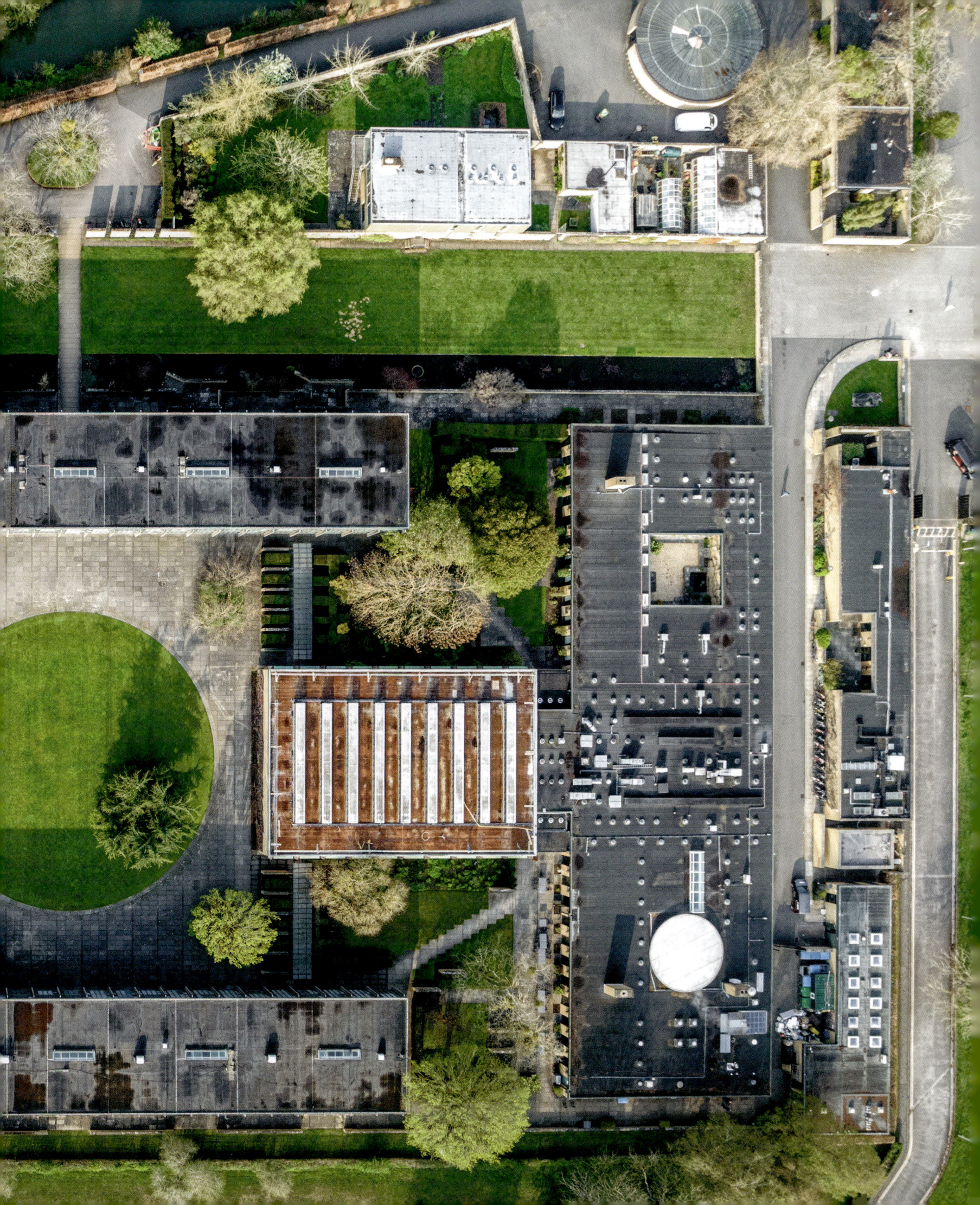

The entire Library space, with service desk, study areas, and bookcases on the ground floor, can be captured in a single gaze from the main entrance. From here, delicate iron stairs lead up to a gallery on the first floor. Along all the exterior walls, this balcony floor is divided into study areas with a cantilevered table that is lit through tall, narrow windows with nature just on the other side. The Library aims to provide the cross-fertilisation of multiple subjects, ranging from mathematics to history.

The Bernard Sunley Lecture Theatre with 208 seats. The lecture theatre was officially opened on 26 October 1966 by Princess Margaret.

St Catherine's layout

6

Despite its simple layout and geometry, St Catherine's possesses the formal character and expressive power expected of a university college. There is clarity in the use of materials: honesty of thought and feeling.

Both lounges are in the Bernard Sunley Building. On the left is the Shaw Room, where the governing body of Catz meets. Below is Room C, which has a variety of uses in the college.

Next spread:

Nothing escapes the rigour of the grid. All construction elements, such as bricks, flashings, doors, windows, paths, flower beds, and even beds fit in precisely. One size fits all. One section in one place is repeated in the same way in other locations.

St Catherine's layout

Monumentality and the beauty of repetition

This and the following two spreads show the beautiful Dining Hall. Jacobsen deftly succeeded in creating a hall with the same air of monumentality and formality that characterises the Dining Halls in other Oxford colleges but without the same sprawling amount of detailing in the ceilings, panels, floors, and furniture.

During the 1960s, many Danish architects found inspiration in Functionalism. By then, Jacobsen belonged to the older generation; in his youth, he had worked extensively with the Functionalist expression. Thus, his use of a late-Modernist expression in St Catherine's is not surprising. That was the way to go to address the demand of incorporating inspiration from classic British university architecture while also pursuing his personal goal of cultivating 'the architectural box as a space and form and played through its precise potentials in a stringent expression'.[140]

St Catherine's is structuralist late Modernism but not the Brutalism characteristic of the time:

There is exposed concrete, but it is never brut.[141]

We see the same recurring feature in several of his later works, including Rødovre Town Hall and Rødovre Library: a main structure consisting of a number of rectangles distributed along a strict axis. A benefit of using simple forms is that they can be arranged in countless (aesthetic) combinations while containing programmes of great complexity. Exactly what a college needs to accommodate its many different disciplines.[142]

140) Thau, C., & Vindum, K. (2002). *Arne Jacobsen* (2nd edition) (p. 167). Arkitektens Forlag.

141) Banham, R. (1964). Criticism: St Catherine's College, Oxford, Churchill College, Cambridge. *The Architectural Review*, 136 (811), 179.

142) 'Structuralism was virtually tailormade for the universities, which were one of the major construction tasks of the welfare society. In Denmark, as in the rest of the Western world, many new universities were being planned around this time.' Andersson, V. M. (2019). *Dansk arkitektur i 1960'erne* (p. 206). Forlaget Rhodos.

The AJ Oxford table lamp from 1963, installed as fixtures.

The key is that 'the box had the potential for monumentality', as Vibeke Andersson Møller explains the paradoxical potential of the simple form.[143] Despite its simple layout and geometry, St Catherine's possesses the formal character and expressive power expected of a university college. There is clarity in the use of materials: honesty of thought and feeling, combined with aesthetic sensibility despite the modest dimensions.[144]

Industrialised architecture had come to Oxford. Diana Rowntree of *The Guardian* described the beauty of repetition in the machine age as 'an arresting beat, and the pattern structure of a Bach fugue'.[145] As she saw it, the potential of the repetition of details on both a large and a small scale would not only serve society, economy, and rational construction but would also per se lead to great architecture.

> *They are usually the work of architects with great individuality [...] the hard edge of the architect's thinking [...] a proliferating cell.*

143) Møller, V.A. (2019). *Dansk arkitektur i 1960'erne*. Forlaget Rhodos, p. 521.

144) Lax, J. (1964, 14 November). Oxford ziggurats: New architecture. *Isis*, 20.

145) Rowntree, D. (1965, 23 June). The beauty of repetition. *The Guardian*.

High Table Dinner. In accordance with Oxford tradition, the students rise when the tutors enter. Everything in the hall was designed by Arne Jacobsen and his studio.

One of the historic elements of Oxford colleges that is clearly present in Catz is the distribution of student rooms around the staircases. In earlier times, too, the students wanted to be able to withdraw for some peace and quiet, even though they lived a communal life, similar to a monastic community.[146] The stairs led up from the garden or yard. If one student wanted to visit another, they would first have to walk down one set of stairs, leave the building and climb another set of stairs. That made for a quieter environment than if the rooms had been placed along a corridor.

146) Randall, A. (1959, 20 March). Traditioner i Oxford. *Berlingske Tidende*, 14.

Fusion of art and architecture

While I was having afternoon tea in the Senior Common Room with photographer Rasmus Hjortshøj, he pointed to a small, colourful rug on the wall next to the fireplace. It looked oddly out of place. Arne Jacobsen believed that his design was complete and required no additional features. Just as he had expressed his explicit concern about the sight of clothes hanging in the student room windows, he was expressly opposed to the idea of covering the interior brick walls with pictures or rugs. Although a small number of preliminary decorations have been added over the years, the people responsible for bringing them in have done so with an anxious glance over their shoulder and a certain sense of guilt, as described by Gervase Rosser, professor of Art History. In response to the question of art and other decorations at Catz, Ainsworth and Howell rhetorically ask, 'Would he [Jacobsen] have seen the works of art added to the walls and gardens as a positive move?' Their own optimistic answer is, 'Hopefully so'.[147] One of the side effects of creating a Gesamtkunstwerk is that anything added to the original work seems out of place. This is the natural result of the combined effects of the synthesis of several art forms.

As Rosser observes in a comment on the visual art and sculptures in Catz, unlike some of the other Oxford colleges, St Catherine's is not a treasure trove of art.[148] Art is intrinsic to the architecture and interior furnishings. Catz was given the offer of borrowing some extremely valuable impressionist paintings by the owner, Richard Walzer, who in 1965 paid for several works by Barbara Hepworth for the Junior Common Room. The college turned down the offer, in part over security concerns, in part over concerns about where to put them.[149] The architecture took precedent over Impressionism.

Lunch in the Senior Common Room at the long table with the elegant, high-backed chairs designed by Jacobsen.

The Senior Common Room with a fireplace and a selection of newspapers and magazines.

Next spread:

The low-ceilinged passage connecting the Senior Common Room and the Dining Hall.

147) Ainsworth, R., & Howell, C. (Eds.) (2012). *St Catherine's, Oxford: A pen portrait* (p. 94). Third Millennium Publishing.
148) Rosser, G. *The Icon of St Catherine in the Library* (Talk for the Senior Common Room), 4 March 2021, p. 1.
149) Davies, M., & Davies, D. (1997). *Creating St Catherine's College* (p. 108). St Catherine's College.

St Catherine's layout

Left, top: The Senior Common Room with the study and the complete model of Catz along the side wall. Left, bottom: the breakfast salon. Right: the passage leading into the lunch room and the room with the fireplace.

A house for music making

The Music House clearly stands out against the rectangular shapes of the rest of the college.

St Catherine's layout

121

The sponsor for the Music House, Hon. Sybil Mary Whitamore, née Borthwick, was the chairwoman of the Women's Liberal Federation in 1955.

The Federation was part of the Liberal Party in Britain and shared and promoted similar ideas about women's role in society.

The brickwork in the Music House still shows the architects' pencil marks indicating the degree of precision they wanted in the laying of the bricks.

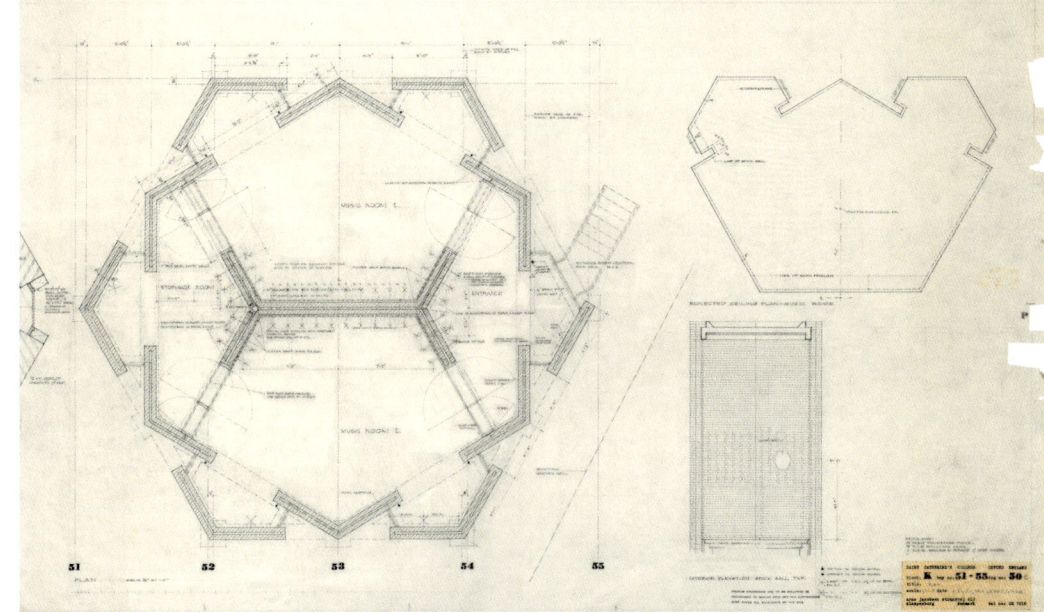

The Music House is located on the west side of the water garden. For acoustic purposes, the interior is designed with staggered spaces. The plan is the original proposal, with an entrance lobby, two practice rooms, and an adjoining store room. This was changed and built as a single performance space occupying the building's entire volume.

Alan Bullock excelled at raising funds for St Catherine's, and the Music House is a particularly illustrative example of his skill.[150] He approached fundraising as a sport:

I enjoyed raising money – it's a curious taste because you've got to put up with the fact that nine times out of ten you don't get anything. But the one you do is fun.[151]

At a reception for another charity project, he met a woman in her seventies who mentioned that she was interested in supporting St Catherine's. He looked into her background and learned from the House of Commons that she was a noblewoman and the daughter of the late Sir Thomas Borthwick. On 31 July 1961, they spoke on the telephone, and in a follow-up letter that same day, Bullock explained that she could either support the general project, which would be going ahead in any case, or she could be the sole donor for a specific building dedicated either to sports – for example, squash courts, a boathouse, or a sports pavilion – or a music house, which would only be built if sufficient external funds could be secured. He estimated that the building would cost about £12,000 and told her she was free to choose its name.

After some discussion with the donor's lawyer concerning the method of payment, a cheque for £13,000 (equivalent to approximately £363,000 in 2024 figures) from Hon. Sybil Mary Whitamore arrived on 5 September 1961.[152] She first saw a model of the building six days later, at a brief, private lunch at the Randolph Hotel, which was all her health allowed, as she suffered from arthritis. Over the following years, she followed up on her engagement in the Music House with a steady flow of characteristic blue handwritten letters from London. In a letter dated 6 September 1962, she inquired how the project was progressing and whether the interior would be modern and dominated by red and yellow? Bullock reassuringly wrote back,

Our architect's tastes are very austere, and I don't think they will run to red and yellow.

Three years after she first heard about the Music House, the building had not yet been completed. In another blue letter, dated 15 May 1964, she wrote rather pointedly,

I am wondering if the 'Powers that be' have decided not to build the 'Music Room' at St. Catherine's.

She expressed frustration because she was unable to give a clear answer when others inquired about the project. On 3 October, she sent three proposals for a plaque in the building, and Bullock chose proposal number 2, which commemorated her parents.

The first concert, an internal event, was held on 26 November 1964, and Bullock made sure to emphasise that this was not a concert hall but 'a house for music making'.

Whitamore ultimately regretted her support. Disappointed over not being invited when Princess Margaret visited St Catherine's and by Alan Bullock's failure to send her a letter of condolence at her brother's passing, in a letter dated 3 November 1967, she expressed her regret and wrote that she would have preferred donating to 'old people's homes'. On behalf of the university, Rodney Shewan diplomatically replied that her donation had secured a permanent source of joy that would not only benefit the young but also senior citizens. The Music House had created a vital cultural tradition 'in a place which has not had time to grow any proper roots'. However, this attempt at reconciliation came too late. Mrs Whitamore had lost interest in St Catherine's.

With its hexagonal shape, placed inside an outer hexagon that has been rotated 45 degrees, the Music House stands out from the general plan and in striking contrast to the rest of the college's right angles and symmetrical layout. Compared to the other buildings, the only influx of daylight comes through the slits in between the two hexagons. The building is set apart on the south-western section of the plot towards the Cherwell and contains a lobby, two rehearsal rooms, and a storage room. A 'riverside folly', as *The Daily Telegraph* described it. The building was awarded the Oxford Preservation Trust Award in 2019.

150) IIIF Box 1. Materials concerning particular College: Music House.

151) Bullock, A. (1984). *How St Catherine's College came to be founded* [A talk given to the Middle Common Room of St Catherine's College on 31 May 1984 by the Founding Master, Lord Bullock of Leafield; verbatim transcript] (p. 38). (LXIC Box: Talks by Lord Bullock and others: Oral history).

152) in2013dollars.com/uk/inflation/1961?amount=13000 (calculated 15 April 2024).

The Master's house

The Master's house is the only element in the original proposal from 1960 that was modified, because Alan Bullock was concerned about noise from the access road.

Next spread:

The east side of the house. The ground level contains the public functions – offices, reception, guest house – and the first floor, the private residence.

The Master's house with a grand piano and with Swan chairs and luminaires designed by Jacobsen.

Along with the bell tower and the Music House, the Master's house also deviates from the strictly defined rectangular layout.[153] On 20 August 1959, when Alan Bullock saw Arne Jacobsen's initial sketches for his new home, his primary wish was to have maximal privacy and to minimise the impact of noise from the access road. To achieve this, he suggested shifting the location of the house on the plot. He sketched out a diagram with arrows showing north and east and two squares with labels marking 'yard, garden, bedroom, study & drawing room'. This simple solution was all it took, he wrote, adding:

> *At the risk of teaching my grandmother to suck eggs, I put in a little sketch on the way in which I think the house should be sited.*

The Master's house and the access road were the only elements to be changed in relation to the initial architectural sketches presented to the public at Brown's Hotel in Mayfair in 1960.[154] When Bullock saw the drawings for the house in February 1961, he was enthusiastic, especially about the idea of using green slate in the reception area. However, he was also worried about the idea of underfloor heating and offered seven suggestions for changes to the design. As this building, too, was subject to cost cuts – from £26,200 to the budgeted £20,000 – the green slate had to go. The end result was a two-storey house with a very clear distribution of functions. All the public spaces were on the ground level, where visiting students were seated in Swan chairs. In addition to the reception area, this level contained the kitchen, larder, dining room, housekeeper's room, and an ensuite guest room that could also be used as a dressing room. Laundry facilities were in the basement, while the private residence was on the first floor.

The Bullock family had accepted that the interior design had to be approved by Arne Jacobsen: the choice and placement of furniture, pictures, curtains, colours, and so forth. Bullock and his wife, Nibby, came from a fully furnished house. As an illustration of Jacobsen's dedication to perfection and obsession with details, the *Daily Mail* printed a story about how the Bullock family struggled to find the right place for their grand piano and sought Jacobsen's advice when he visited. Under a photo of the architect, engineer Ove Arup, and Bullock, the paper wrote that Jacobsen and Bullock had wheeled the grand piano round the place, until the architect found the right place for it: at the window.

---

153) IIIF Box 1. Materials concerning particular College: *Master's House*; Rosenfield, R. (1964, 24 July). The Master's home suits his wife. *Oxford Mail*, 3; Rosenfield, R. (1964, 24 July). Field wanted. *Oxford Mail*, 3.

154) Bullock, A. (1984). *How St Catherine's College came to be founded* [A talk given to the Middle Common Room of St Catherine's College on 31 May 1984 by the Founding Master, Lord Bullock of Leafield; verbatim transcript] (p. 29). (LXIC Box: Talks by Lord Bullock and others: Oral history).

The 42 strokes of the bell

Antique Japanese bells, known as tsurigane, meaning 'hanging bells', are still in use today in Buddhist temples all over Japan. They are often struck from the outside using a beam suspended from a rope. They have a low pitch and a deep resonance that can last up to a minute. They are typically cast in bronze and decorated with horizontal bands, kanji characters, or inscriptions.

Opposite page:

The bell tower is an indispensable vertical landmark. Every evening, the bell rings out with 41 or 42 strokes.

Next spread:

Regardless of the ascetic architectural expression, Catz appears with a high degree of variation depending on the natural light and the time of day.

In order to keep costs down, an effort was made to acquire one or two used bells for the bell tower, provided the sound was satisfactory.[155] In a handwritten letter dated 26 October 1962, Peter C. Swann of the Ashmolean Museum had two suggestions. One was to acquire a Japanese bell from the Obelisk Gallery, in London's Crawford Street, dating from 1301, measuring 2.7 feet in height and weighing 224–336 pounds (2–3 CWT).[156] The gallery was asking £200 for the bell; Swann offered £100.

His other suggestion involved four Japanese bronze bells owned by the Victoria and Albert Museum in London. The V&A director, Sir Trenchard Cox, was willing to lend one of the four bells to the college. At 10:30 am on 15 January 1963, Jack Lankester, project manager and the university's surveyor, visited the museum to see the bells for himself.

The visit was a success. The following day, Lankester thanked the museum for the meeting and asked if the bells could be lifted down off their stands to allow himself and Swann to hear their sound at an upcoming meeting on Tuesday 5 February. Only the smallest of the bells, dating from 1847, was made available in this way. It weighed 496 pounds (4 CWT 48 lb) and was 4.5 feet high, with a base diameter of 24.8 inches.

However, in a shock announcement, the building committee declared that it wanted to cut costs by either postponing or cancelling the construction of the bell tower. Upon hearing this, Lankester wrote to Alan Bullock on 5 March 1963, venting his frustration in explicit terms. In his opinion, there was no financial incentive to postpone the construction, since the builders were on site, ready to start, and would be entitled to compensation:

A decision to abandon the tower would in my view be aesthetically disastrous and would destroy the unity of a design that is incomplete without such a vertical feature.

He also had a personal motivation to see the bell tower erected. In a meeting with Arne Jacobsen in Copenhagen to find cuts of £180,000, he had given his word that even though the tower was not a functional necessity, it would not be cut:

I would feel very upset if we now went back on it.

His disappointment and deepfelt desperation are palpable, and in the following draft budgets for the respective scenarios, he exaggerated the estimates by one or two thirds.

The main contractor, Marshall-Andrew, sent an estimate of £2,973 for the new tower, compared to the original estimate of just £481. According to the contractor, the sixfold increase occurred because the new design included many more components, which greatly added to the complexity of the task. Jack Lankester then wrote to Jacobsen to explain that if the tower were to be realised, he would have to revert to the original design in order to bind the contractor to the original price.

155) IIIF Box 1. Materials concerning particular College: *Bell Tower*.
156) CWT stands for 'a hundredweight', a British measure equal to 112 pounds or 50.8 kilos. investopedia.com/terms/h/hundredweight.asp

St Catherine's layout

Six days later, Lankester had Jacobsen's reply:

It is very much to regret that every time we try to do something to make the quality better, we are stopped [...]. In my opinion it is extremely important that the college will not be without tower for a longer period, and consequently we have to accept a poorer quality.

Although Jacobsen was unhappy about having to compromise, it was a condition for saving the tower.

The Japanese bell was now transported to the Whitechapel Bell Foundry in London to be prepared for installation. However, when the bell was tested, it was found to have no 'breath'. The experts at the foundry suspected an invisible crack – which proved to be the case. The promising solution would have to be abandoned. Douglas Hughes from the foundry wrote on 19 December 1963:

I cannot see how this bell can possibly be hung in a tower and used for calling people to worship.

At St Catherine's, there was deep disappointment, as the idea of the Japanese bell had seemed very appealing. However, rather than risking the use of bell that might split in two, the choice was made to install a simple English bell weighing 336 pounds (3 CWT), measuring 24 inches in diameter, and tuned to the note of G.

That is the bell that is still in use today. Every night at 7.05 pm, it strikes 42 strokes. But why this exact time and why the unusual number of strokes? The answer has both technical and historical aspects. Originally, the Porter's Lodge was located on the ground level of staircase 14, in the middle of the western accommodation block. At the time, the bell was operated by a porter who manually started it with the push of a button and stopped it in the same way a minute later.

When the decision was made to move the Porter's Lodge to the building by the new northern entrance, the bell could no longer be operated via a simple, directly cabled on/off switch. Instead, a network-controlled system was installed.

The reason why the bell begins to ring at 7:05 pm, rather than at 7:15 pm when dinner begins in the Dining Hall, is that the bell is intended to remind diners that it is time to go to dinner, rather than announcing that dinner has been served. The bell is not specifically programmed to strike 42 times; that is simply the number of strokes the original mechanism from the 1960s can produce in one minute before the bell mechanism is powered off.

The very pale, mechanical brickwork, walls of glass, and perfect concrete surfaces made you think your fingers might go dead if they touched them.

There are no quarter or half closures (bats).

The flooring in the Dining Hall is green slate from Broughton Moor, which Arne Jacobsen liked so much that he had a circular tabletop measuring 3.6 feet by 1.18 inches made for himself. Originally, Jacobsen had wanted Porsgrunn marble from Telemarken, Norway: the same type he used in Søllerød Town Hall. That would have been more practical and also cheaper, because the production of the slate using fairly primitive machinery led to a large amount of waste, which added to the cost. According to Bullock's memoirs, Bullock opposed the idea of marble: 'My God, what do you think we are, this isn't the Renaissance.'

Next spread:

The horizontal slats on the exterior of the Bernard Sunley Building create an interplay of light and shadows on the wall.

Bricks, columns, and girders

What raises Catz above Modernism's potential boredom, Structuralism's repetition, and Brutalism's stern use of materials is both the recurring use of ochre-coloured, tactile, three-dimensional brickwork and the polished surface of the concrete in the beams and cruciform columns. The brick has a similar glow to the sandstone used in Oxford's historic colleges, libraries, hotels, and houses as well as the villages around it, for example Iffley and Woodstock. The sandstone defines the image of Oxford. As an added subtlety, the edges of the columns and beams are slightly chamfered, which lends the concrete a softer visual expression and tactile feel. They were cast in precisely executed wooden moulds without visual seams and with an interior surface of smooth, waterproof polyurethane lacquer,[157] but not everyone was a fan of the clear materiality:

The very pale, mechanical brickwork, walls of glass, and perfect concrete surfaces made you think your fingers might go dead if they touched them.[158]

In his memoirs, Jack Lankester, the university architect, wrote about the bricks and the general shortage of building materials in the 1950s and early 1960s.[159] Brick production had yet to resume fully after the war, and the industry was changing due to the growing popularity of prefab construction systems and so-called curtain walls, a facade element that is fixed to the load-bearing construction but is not load-bearing in itself. When Jacobsen needed bricks, they were in very short supply. He wanted bricks made of natural clay due to its superior wearability, 2 inches thick (about 5.1 centimetres and the Danish standard size), rather than the British standard size of 2 5/8 inches (about 6.7 centimetres) and in a pale, yellowish brown. Only a few manufacturers made bricks of these dimensions, and even fewer could deliver the desired colour. Only one company, Cape Building Products Ltd. in Uxbridge, made a brick that came close to the specifications: the 2-inch Uxbridge flint brick, which was dyed using yellow iron hydrate from Golden Valley Co. in Wales.[160]

In this context, the use of this particular brick plays an active visual role. Normally, the vertical joint in a brick bond comes up to the middle of the brick above and below.

At St Catherine's, the distance is only a quarter of the brick below, and thus, even the slightest imprecision becomes visible. The use of the slender brick with a deep-set joint prevents the low walls in the garden, for example, from looking stout. To this day, you can see pencil marks on the bricks showing the degree of precision the architects called for and how hard it was for the bricklayers to accomplish it. The maximum rate for a bricklayer was 15 bricks an hour.[161] Generally, the fastest rate could be achieved in the construction of retaining walls, where most of the brickwork is not exposed, for example in 19th-century railway viaducts, when construction probably proceeded at a rate of 2,000 bricks per day.

Former student Peter Green (Zoology) recollected how the bricklayers – many of whom were low-income workers from Ireland – were 'princes' among the builders on the site, while the brickies' labourers – the hod carriers – who moved the bricks and mortar (colloquially called muck), were 'princes' among the workers.[162] Their backbreaking, painstaking work earned them the place at the top of their respective hierarchies.

---

157) LXIC Box: Talks by Lord Bullock and others. Oral history 3_ Margaret Davies talk for C20 Society2002Library architecture at Oxford-St Catherine's College, pp. 8–9.

158) Gardiner, S. Changing Masterpiece. *The Observer*. (IIJ Box 8_9_Magazine articles).

159) IIJ Box 1_The Architect-appointment-note by Lord Bullock – correspondence: 3_Correspondence on choice of architect, 1958.

160) Correspondence with Arne Jacobsen on 10 November 1960. St. Catherine's College Oxford. Danish National Archives (Business Archive). Correspondence 1963, 1964 (283); Correspondence with engineer Dürkopp on 20 May 1965. St. Catherine's College Oxford. Danish National Archives (Business Archive). Correspondence 1965, 1968 (285).

161) IIJ Box 1_6 Lord Bullock. Correspondence between Jack Lankester and Derek Davies.

162) Green, P. (2012). Memoirs of an idle labourer – or how I built my own college. In R. Ainsworth & C. Howell (Eds.) (2012). *St Catherine's, Oxford: A pen portrait* (p. 162). Third Millennium Publishing.

St Catherine's layout

❛
Naturally, Jacobsen had a profound passion for architecture, but it was his love of nature and painting that brought him happiness.

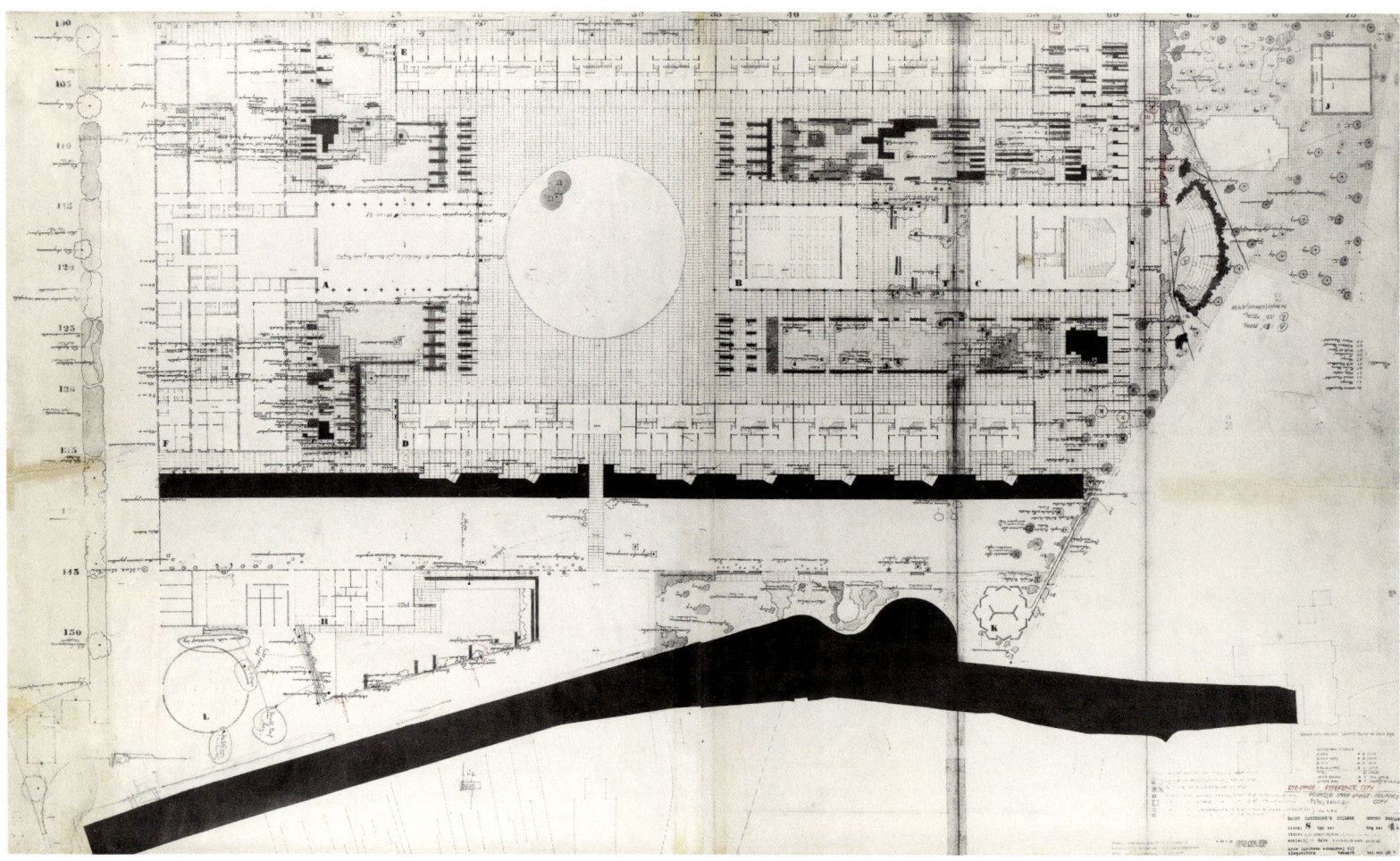

Fusion of architecture and landscape

For years, the original garden plan was presumed lost. However, it was found intact in the RIBA Drawings Collection (to which it had been donated by Peter Denney from his personal collection of drawings of the college).

Two impulses governed Jacobsen's extraordinary career. One was a love of nature – he studied trees and plants in depth throughout his life. The other was a strong interest in painting and sculpture.[163]

This was how *Design Week*, in 1988, summed up the essence of the artistic sensibilities that ran through an entire career. Naturally, Jacobsen had a profound passion for architecture, but it was his love of nature and painting that brought him happiness. In his architecture, he placed particular emphasis on 'sensitivity to the artistic side of the matter', as he put it.[164]

Jacobsen had drawn up a list of 758 species of plants and shrubs that he wanted to include in the gardens around Catz.[165] As in his landscape design for Søllerød Town Hall, he favoured bamboo and planned to use it rather extensively,[166] in part because, in his assessment, Britain had a wider variety of bamboo than was available in Denmark.

The initial garden plan was prepared in his studio in Klampenborg between May and October 1962. It is painstakingly detailed and includes Jacobsen's handwritten labels for every single shrub and tree – upside down in relation to the orientation of the plan. In his recollections about the establishment of the garden, Garden Master Barrie Juniper wrote that Jacobsen's original garden plan seemed to have disappeared.[167] Fortunately, that is not the case; it is part of the RIBA archives in London, and as far as I have been able to ascertain, it has never before been published.

The establishment of the garden began in the winter of 1963–64 and was largely completed by 1968. The first Lebanese cedar on the Quad was 35 feet tall.[168] It was moved 2 miles from a private address in North Oxford to St Catherine's on 20

---

163) Myerson, J. (1988, 6 May). The art of Arne Jacobsen. *Design Week*. (Box 8_9_15 Magazine articles).
164) Ninka (1971, 28 February). Det nye kritiseres altid [The new is always criticised]. *Politiken*, 13.
165) Arne Jacobsen i Oxford. (1963, 18 July). *Berlingske Aftenavis*, 4.
166) VIB Box 1: Early plans and correspondence about planning and planting the garden.
167) Juniper, B. (2012). The gardens. In R. Ainsworth & C. Howell (Eds.), *St Catherine's, Oxford: A pen portrait* (p. 74). Third Millennium Publishing.
168) A tree's journey through Oxford. (1964, 21 April). *Oxford Mail*.

The Quad is a popular area among the students, as it forms the setting of countless informal encounters.

Next spread:

The heart of Catz is the Quad, which extends between the Dining Hall on the right and the Library on the left.

April 1964 on a platform truck during rush hour. It took five hours, with police escort. Before it was transplanted, the tree had been personally approved by Jacobsen.

The tree did not survive the winter. In a letter dated 19 October 1965, Arne Jacobsen requested another tree measuring at least 24 feet, because the scale of the space called for a mature tree.[169] On the other hand, he did not wish to repeat the experiment, so this time, he asked for a younger tree that had been prepared for two years. It arrived in March 1966 and was a semi-mature tree from the Rothschild Estate near Exbury.[170]

Jacobsen's original plan from 1962 seems to show two trees, and in fact, on several occasions, it was debated whether there should be two. Jacobsen liked the idea, provided that the distance between them was no more than 35 feet.[171] The Quad has had four cedar trees in total. The third tree, a three-year-old specimen, was planted in February 1972, and Garden Master Barrie Juniper actually mentioned two in his 1980 guide book.[172] The oldest was cut down in December 1999, the other one in 2010, while the current tree, a genuine Lebanese cedar tree, was planted in 2000.[173]

Like the buildings, the garden was designed in a strict grid on a north-south axis. This includes the rectangular water garden with the terraces that runs the full length of the area on the west side, interrupted only by the former main entrance. The long inner lawn between the student accommodation blocks extends both north and south of the central Quad and is dominated by parallel sections of wall interspersed with yew hedges of the same height as the walls. Towards the north, off the Senior and Junior Common Rooms, there are semiprivate gardens surrounded by buildings. Towards the south, there is an amphitheatre with concrete steps, surrounded by sculpted yews. All the trees in the plan are planted as solitaries in between the accommodation blocks, the lecture theatre, and the south section of the college, which provides ideal conditions for balanced, imposing crowns.

171) Undated letter from Peter Denney to the Bursar. VIB Box 2: Correspondence about planning and planting the garden.
172) Juniper, B. (1980). *A guide to the gardens of St Catherine's College, Oxford* (p. 7). St Catherine's College.
173) Henfrey, A. W. (2012). The cedar tree: A long story with a happy ending. In R. Ainsworth & C. Howell (Eds.), *St Catherine's, Oxford: A pen portrait* (pp. 82–83). Third Millennium Publishing.

169) VIC Box. Trees in the Quadrangle.
170) This information comes from notes by Garden Master Barrie Juniper on the garden plan of 1972.

St Catherine's layout

Mistakes in the garden plan

Left: The garden in its initial stage in the early 1960s, photographed from the roof above the Senior Common Room. Right: The mature garden, same place, 60 years later.

St Catherine's was built and established in many stages, which led to numerous additions and adjustments. This includes the original garden plan. In 1972 – the year after Jacobsen's death – Garden Master Barrie Juniper carried out a careful inventory of the plants in the garden, which corresponds much more closely with reality than the original plan does. The flowering season in the garden aims for two climaxes: May–June and October. Catz's Archives also contain two meticulous inventories, made by Barrie Juniper in 1983, of the plants that bloom in summer and autumn respectively, including ornamental flowers, fruit, or leaves. The list includes 26 trees (all year), 40 plants that bloom in autumn (June–December), 84 plants that bloom in summer (May–October), and 31 hedges (May–August).

However, Jacobsen almost made a mistake in his garden plan. Among other plants, he wanted rhododendrons and heather, but both are acidophile plants, which need a pH value between 4.5 and 5.5, while the soil at Catz (measured in 1995) has a pH value of 6.5 (only slightly acidic) and is moist and rich in calcium.[174] Three factors made the site unsuitable for heather and rhododendrons:

1. The soil was too heavy and calcareous.

2. The cost of replacing or treating the soil would be excessive, and such treatment would need to be repeated over and over.

3. Some of the plants were not hardy enough to survive a hard winter in the Oxford climate and would need to be protected from frost and the damp winter weather.

Over the coming months, Juniper met privately with Jacobsen to adjust the vegetation to match the soil.[175] During the many hours the two men spent together, Juniper realised that Jacobsen detested flowers, finding them too small and dainty in a college of this scale. Still, Bullock

174) Plougsgaard, H. (2012, 4 August). Danske spor i Oxford. *Morgenavisen Jyllands-Posten*; Cooper, L. (2003). *The gardens of St Catherine's College, Oxford: A review – with the future in mind* [draft dissertation], Appendix 1.

175) Jacobsen's extensive knowledge about plants is reflected in an internal note from November 1963 to Alan Bullock, in which Juniper explains that he and Jacobsen had now drawn the preliminary design of the vestibule gardens: 'Some of the items Professor Jacobsen asked for are not easy to obtain but the Botanic Garden has offered to help in giving plants where they cannot be bought.' VIB Box 1: Early plans and correspondence about planning and planting the garden.

plucked up his courage, and in a garden meeting on 5 June 1964, he asked Knud Holscher for a flower bed on the Quad. To advocate for it, he hid behind the English Prince Consort: 'Prince Philip felt that the place looked like a prison.'[176]

Instead, Jacobsen had a weakness for trees, tree shapes, and leaf textures: in short, trees throughout the seasons. In a draft for an article, Juniper concluded: 'And he was right. In a contrived landscape, melding into the natural vista of lower Thames water meadow, fussy little flower beds of municipal planting would have looked ridiculous'.[177] Notwithstanding the replacements of individual trees and hedges, modifications to accommodate the new entrance and modifications of several courtyard gardens, such as the Helen Gaskin Memorial Garden, Juniper comments in an undated letter that '[t]he basic skeleton of Arne Jacobsen's original garden design remains'.[178]

In 1970, he wrote:

Such a design is compatible with modern English ideas of gardening, slowly escaping from the expensive tyranny of summer bedding.[179]

As he explained, college grounds and gardens are not just intended for visual decoration but should provide the same sense of peace and calm as a private back garden. The real walls of a college are the flesh, blood, and intellect of young people. One day, life will catch up with them, and they will leave, taking the most important baggage with them: the knowledge they have gained. Hence, the setting for their lives should be sturdy enough to be left out at night and fit to be an active participant in their activities and education.

176) Danish National Archives (Business Archive). Correspondence 1964, 1965 (284).
177) Juniper, B. (2011). *The building of the Garden* [draft of 2012 book chapter on gardens). VIE Box. 'Reminiscences' of Garden Master (B.E.J.).
178) Ibid.
179) Juniper, B. (1969–70). The Garden of St Catherine's College, Oxford. *St Catherine's Chronicle*, *Oxford*, 14–15.

Oxford staged

Left: The now fully grown garden behind the Senior Common Room.

Right: The amphitheatre. Jacobsen altered the hedge line to the right and left sides of the amphitheatre from the original plan to ensure that the spectators would not be visible from the approach to the Lecture Theatre – a sophisticated detail with great architectural significance.

The use of parallel walls interspersed with yew hedges is a striking feature of the garden plan.[180] It lends the garden a spatial, theatrical, and labyrinthine effect that has been a part of landscaping for centuries. Jacobsen also used this concept in his own garden in Klampenborg, north of Copenhagen, where the hedges provided shelter and subdivided the garden space, as he explained in the Danish TV programme *Arne Jacobsen in Oxford*.[181] Landscape designer Louise Cooper suggests that he may have been inspired by the Lasker Rose Garden by Sylvia Crowe (1953) in the Oxford Botanic Garden, just south of St Catherine's, whose rose beds are surrounded by a labyrinthine pattern of low rectangular yew hedges.[182]

In any case, Jacobsen's design is not characterised by the denial of historical tradition that was common in Modernist gardens and landscapes until the early 1960s. At Catz, the garden was a building component of equal significance as the architecture that embraced it. Without Jacobsen's extensive knowledge about plants, the buildings might have verged on the boring. Generally, in this type of garden design, 'the garden in its classical role modulates the passage from geometry to nature and anchors the house firmly to the ground'.[183]

The multifaceted fusion of architecture and landscape reflects the enigmatic complexities of the city of Oxford: unexpected glimpses, crooked lanes, disappearing panoramas, and – in some places – surprisingly generous spaces. Throughout, there is great contrast between inside and out. Oxford is a city of walls enclosing secret worlds of green lawns, fountains, and historic buildings sheltered from the noise of busy streets but providing access to visitors through rare entrances in solid walls.[184]

The eye is led to glimpses of grass through foliage; colonnades are transformed into leafy tunnels; tall brick walls vanish behind creepers. St. Catherine's is a kind of masterpiece which, unlike a painting, will always be changing, and improving.[185]

It is difficult to separate architecture and landscape, since it is in the fusion of inside and outside that we discover the codes for the structure and inherent logic of the place.

180) Craig, S. P. (1995). *A Guide to the gardens of St Catherine's College Oxford* (p. 1). St Catherine's College; Brown, J. (2000). *The modern garden* (pp. 176–178). Thames & Hudson.
181) Dreyer, O. (Director). (1970). *Arne Jacobsen i Oxford* [TV documentary]. DR. See also Sheridan, M. (2023). *Room 606: The SAS house and the work of Arne Jacobsen* (pp. 192–193). Strandberg Publishing.
182) Cooper, L. (2003). *The gardens of St Catherine's College, Oxford: A review – with the future in mind*, Appendix 1 (p. 36). [Draft dissertation]

183) de Wit, S. (2018). *Hidden Landscapes: The metropolitan garden as a multi-sensory expression of place* (p. 36). Architectura & Natura.

184) Browne, K. (1977). Eyehold on Oxford... combination of fine buildings into a townscape. *The Architectural Review*, 162(970), 341.
185) Gardiner, S. Changing Masterpiece. *The Observer*. (Box 8_9_14 Magazine articles).

The walls also help to break up the wind in the fairly large garden and on the Quad.

St Catherine's layout

Jacobsen was proven right. What were empty spaces in 1964 are now populated by tall trees, hedges, and lawns.

Wait for the landscape

Catz has a monastic asceticism. Visitors have to go past the circular bike shed before they see the western-most accommodation block on a flat lawn with a rectangular strip of water and the Barbara Hepworth sculpture.

'Before you criticise my building, wait for the landscape to appear,' Arne Jacobsen said to *The Observer* at the official opening in 1964. In another piece, the same newspaper argued that 'now is the time to see it, when it is the hardest to like. This is how the Renaissance must have hit the Gothic-softened burghers of earlier England'.[186] But Jacobsen was proven right. What were empty spaces in 1964 are now populated by lawns and tall trees and hidden behind high, green bands of dense hedges and parallel walls of ochre-coloured limestone and sandstone. The extensive correspondence about the plantings show that Jacobsen went into every detail, including the yew hedges for Alan Bullock's garden and his thuja hedge, which appeared to be on its last legs.[187]

The buildings were Grade I listed in 1994, as the only college that year and as one of only five postwar listings, and the garden was assigned a Grade II listing in 1998 as one of 12 listed college gardens in Oxford. This marked the official recognition of Catz as a site of international historic and architectural significance at the same level as Britain's medieval cathedrals.[188]

186) Manser, M. (1964, 26 July). The Oxbridge double. *The Observer*. (IIJ Box _9_1).

187) Correspondence with Peter Denney, 21 May 1965. St. Catherine's College Oxford. Danish National Archives (Business Archive). Correspondence 1965, 1968 (285).
188) Mr Macmillan praises a great Dane. (1964, 17 October). *The Guardian*.

An efficient, altruistic man

Alan Bullock also played a key role in fundraising and networking to make the garden possible.[189] As early as in 1957, he contacted Jessie B. Coulthurst of the Coulthurst Trust to propose that the trust might fund a modern, simple chapel with room for 150–200 worshippers. In his estimate, the cost of such a chapel would not exceed £25,000–30,000, while building a first-class organ would cost £10,000–15,000. It is noteworthy that in addition to seeking substantial funds for the college itself, in many cases he also intervened on behalf of students who, for one reason or another, had fallen on hard times and were struggling to come up with enough money to finish their studies. Whether this was an Orthodox-Jewish Israeli student or a young American whose uncle had suffered a business setback, he insisted on looking out for them. To this day, there is a £250 cheque in the Catz archives that was never cashed.

The chapel was the ideal showcase, Bullock felt, for the trust to invest in, as the grant would be earmarked for a specific purpose that could only be realised if sufficient external funds were secured. Ultimately, however, the chapel was not built. It was included in the original plans, sited east of the amphitheatre, but was left out in order to cut costs, in part on the recommendations of the teaching staff.[190] This makes Catz one of the few Oxford colleges not to have a chapel.

Instead, some members of the college frequented Holywell Church – now St Cross – a medieval village church located on the corner of St Catherine's site.[191] Today, it houses a stunningly beautiful archive of historical papers belonging to Balliol College, which rents the building from the Church of England on a 999-year lease.[192]

189) VIA Box: *The College gardens*.

190) Davies, M., & Davies, D. (1997). *Creating St Catherine's College* (pp. 68–69). St Catherine's College.

191) Lack, A. (2009). New role for St Cross. *Oxfordshire Limited Edition*, 79.

192) *St Cross Church, Holywell: Its history, architecture, people, and conversion into an Historic Collections Centre* (p. 20) (2011). Balliol College Oxford.

Holywell Church, now St Cross, is one of hundreds of churches in Britain that have been deconsecrated and put to new uses. St Cross would be fairly easy to turn back into a church. There is still a large number of graves around the former church.

The garden behind the Junior Common Room.

The decision not to include a college chapel may have roots in the liberal and open-minded line at Catz, where it was also debated whether the Music House might be used for religious purposes, at least occasionally.[193]

Let us now rewind to 1 July 1959, when Bullock was delighted to share with Jessie B. Coulthurst that he had now raised the staggering sum of £1,323,000, no doubt because he was hoping that the success of the project might impress her enough to make her want to join in. Eight days later, he proposed two additional possibilities: Coulthurst could either contribute with guest residences for future visiting scholars, a programme to which the Rockefeller Foundation had donated £100,000 in order to boost St Catherine's during its initial years. Or the trust could contribute to the garden:

Jacobsen has a big reputation as a landscape architect and we have commissioned him to lay out the garden and grounds in addition to designing the buildings.

Coulthurst chose the garden and offered to pay £20,000 for planting trees, flowers, and shrubs and establishing lawns and another £15,000 for maintenance of the grounds. In the end, the trust contributed a total of £50,000, half in cash and the rest in securities. In addition to funds, Coulthurst also offered opinions about the buildings, which she felt should have been taller. Since space was in short supply, building high was the only option. She was concerned for the students' access to affordable housing and whether they were properly fed without needing to take student jobs when they should be focusing fully on their studies: 'Wonder how many lock up Garages (sic) are being provided in the scheme,' she wrote.

[193] 'If it were no longer available as a church, few would notice the loss.' Handwritten letter from Derek Davies dated 6 November 1986 during the negotiations about a possible takeover of St Cross. (VIIIA Box: Chaplaincy and religious matters).

St Catherine's layout

Two sports grounds were never realised

Merton College wanted to move their sports grounds to the site next to St Catherine's when their existing facilities were closed down. Most colleges in Oxford and Cambridge have their own sports grounds, since sport is considered a crucial aspect of personal growth – from young people to seasoned leaders. On the pitch or on the court, people discover how they react when they lose. Sport builds character and provides self-insight.

On 8 August 1963, the bursar of Merton College, R. B. C. Hodgson, wrote to Jacobsen in Denmark to ask if he and his firm would act as the college's architect.[194] Merton was a small college with 200 bachelor students, and after talks with Knud Holscher, it wanted to add a pavilion with a kitchen, storage space, changing rooms, and showers for 50 men and 5 women constructed as a one-storey structure with a flat roof (second draft). The project would also include a 1290-square-foot home for the gardener, a car park and bike store with room for 40 cars and 50 bicycles as well as four squash courts and, at a later date, a swimming pool. The project was to be completed in 1965–1966.

Jacobsen accepted the project. He and Holscher met with the building committee on 20 March 1964 to debate the architects' drafts and a handwritten estimate of £123,000. However, St Catherine's was also looking to build its own sports grounds, right next to Merton's, so on 19 August 1964, Jacobsen asked R. B. C. Hodgson for permission to consider the proposals jointly and to share Merton's building programme with St Catherine's in order to help the latter determine their own needs.

In 1964, St Catherine's bursar, D. J. Wenden, was in negotiations with both Merton College and the planning department of the City of Oxford to buy the plot north of the new college and therefore asked Jacobsen's firm to prepare drawings of the facility. The plan was to have facilities for football (soccer), cricket, hockey, and parking, as well as a pavilion and, perhaps at a later time, tennis courts. The drawings were prepared in September.

Ultimately, neither project was realised. On 14 October 1964, R. B. C. Hodgson dismissed Arne Jacobsen, stating that neither the first project, from March, nor the revised project, from August 1964, had met the college's expectations. However, Hodgson assured Jacobsen that this decision would have no impact on St Catherine's continued efforts to establish their sports facilities on the neighbouring plot.

In a letter to Merton dated 2 January 1965, Jacobsen explained that given the new information from both colleges, he had no choice but to annul the previous proposals. His disappointment is evident in the letter. He had understood his commission to mean that he would continue work from the neighbouring college, aiming to create a design that was in harmony with the new builds in mass and layout but which also, and thanks to the different characters of the programmes, had its own distinct identity: 'I have wasted your committee's time as well as my own.'

However, the perspective and plans reveal where and how the intended grounds were to be incorporated into the geometry of the existing structures at St Catherine's. The negotiations with Merton College about buying the northern plot as a space for sports and parking continued until October 1966, and it was a tough process.[195] Merton's objections all revolved around the same main issues: concerns about lacking free and unhindered access to their own sports grounds and the inconvenience of needing to cross over St Catherine's land to enter their own grounds. The ultimate dealbreaker was the duration of the lease that Merton was willing to offer.[196]

Merton College Sports Pavilion, on the other hand, was realised in 1974, designed by architect Michael Dixey. Today, this pavilion is Grade II listed and surrounded by sports pitches, tennis and squash courts, and weight-training facilities. The plans for sports grounds for St Catherine's were never realised. Nevertheless, Catz has produced both male and female Olympic and World Cup medallists and contributed to the national sports associations.[197]

194) Danish National Archives (Business Archive). Correspondence 1964, 1965 (284).
195) Letter from Alan Bullock to Arne Jacobsen dated 24 October.1966. Danish National Archives (Business Archive). Correspondence 1965, 1968 (285).
196) Davies, M., & Davies, D. (1997). *Creating St Catherine's College* (p. 74). St Catherine's College.
197) Ainsworth, R., & Howell, C. (Eds.) (2012). *St Catherine's, Oxford: A pen portrait* (p. 148). Third Millennium Publishing.

Perspective draft seen from the south showing the sports pavilion at Merton College. There are clear references to the pragmatism of the St Catherine's grid.

Unrealised projects: sports grounds at Catz and Merton.

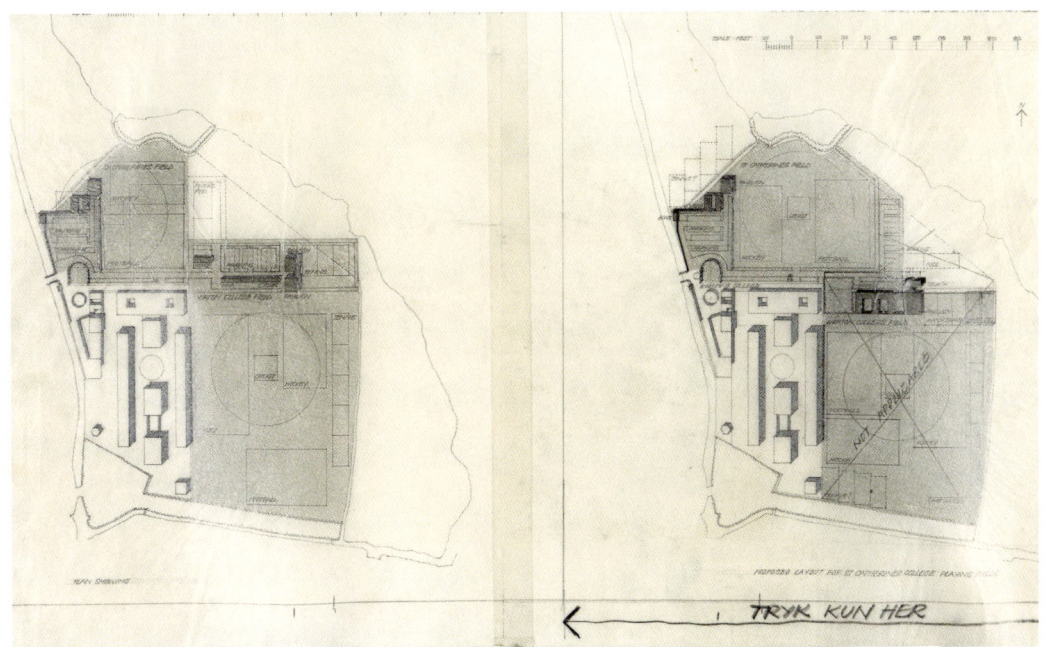

A previously unpublished perspective of the sports grounds at Catz, signed by Jacobsen in March 1966. The drawing shows how he envisioned future extensions. The new buildings by Stephen Hodder and Purcell adhere closely to this vision. See map on page 12.

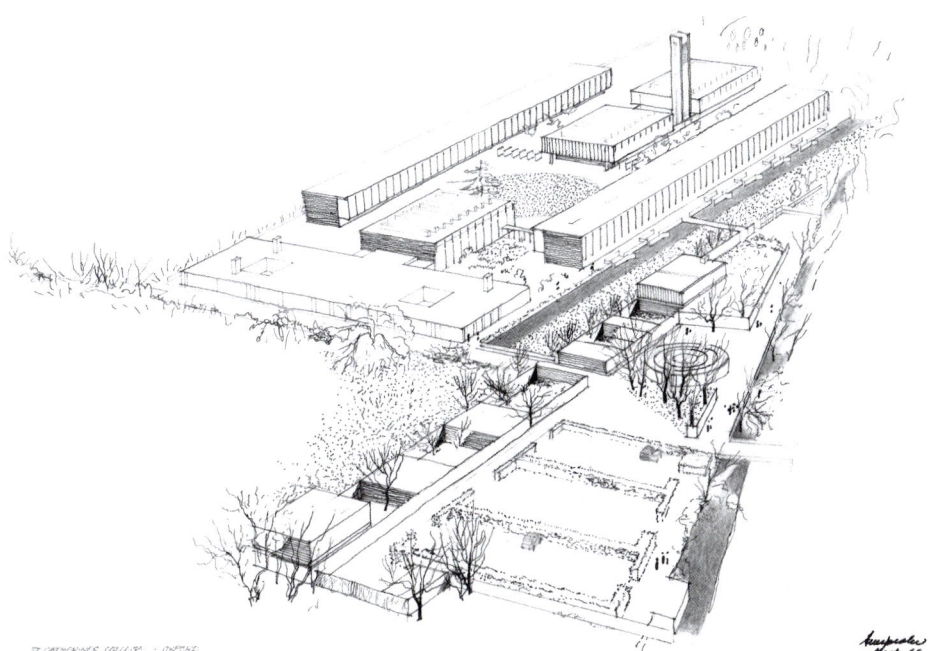

Throughout, the work is dominated by a simple and consistent idea that leaves room for both artistic and pragmatic solutions.

St Catherine's layout

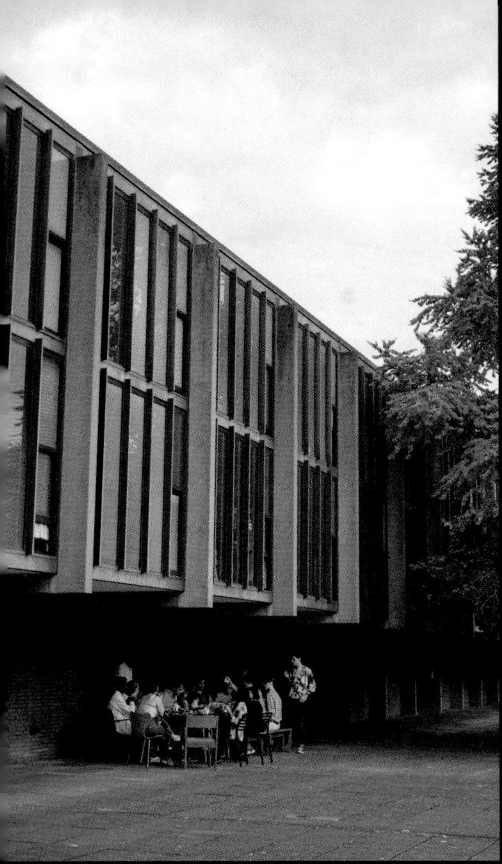
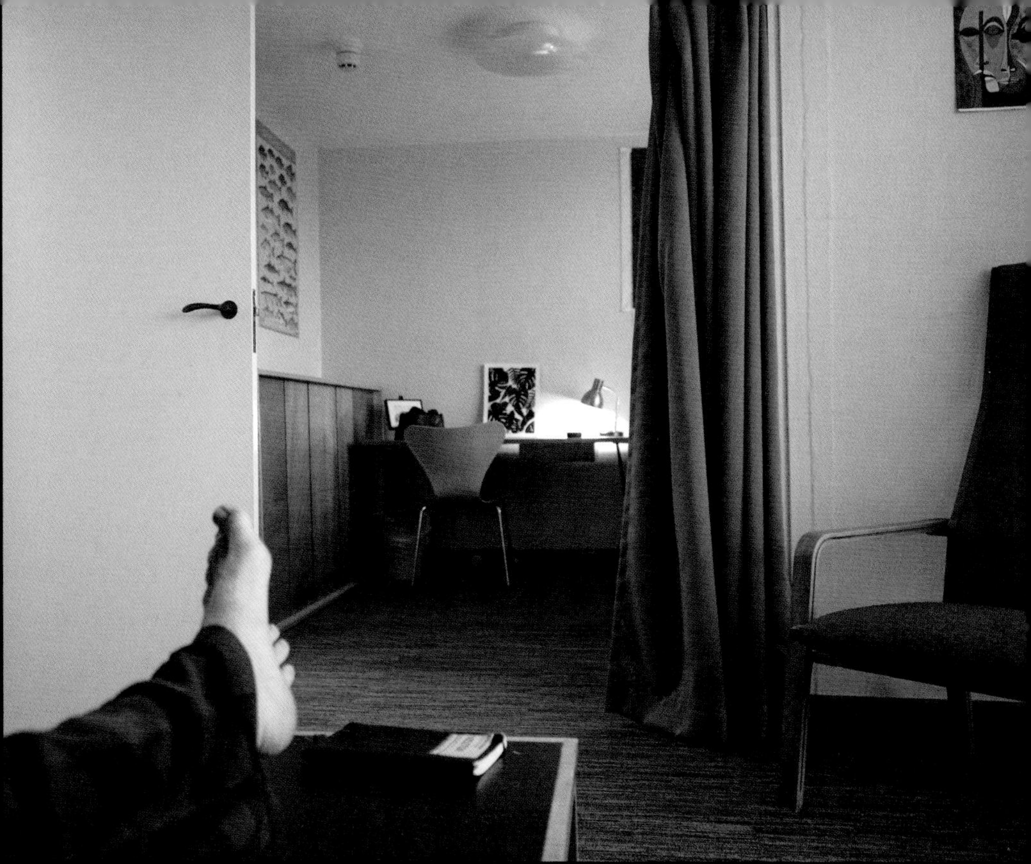
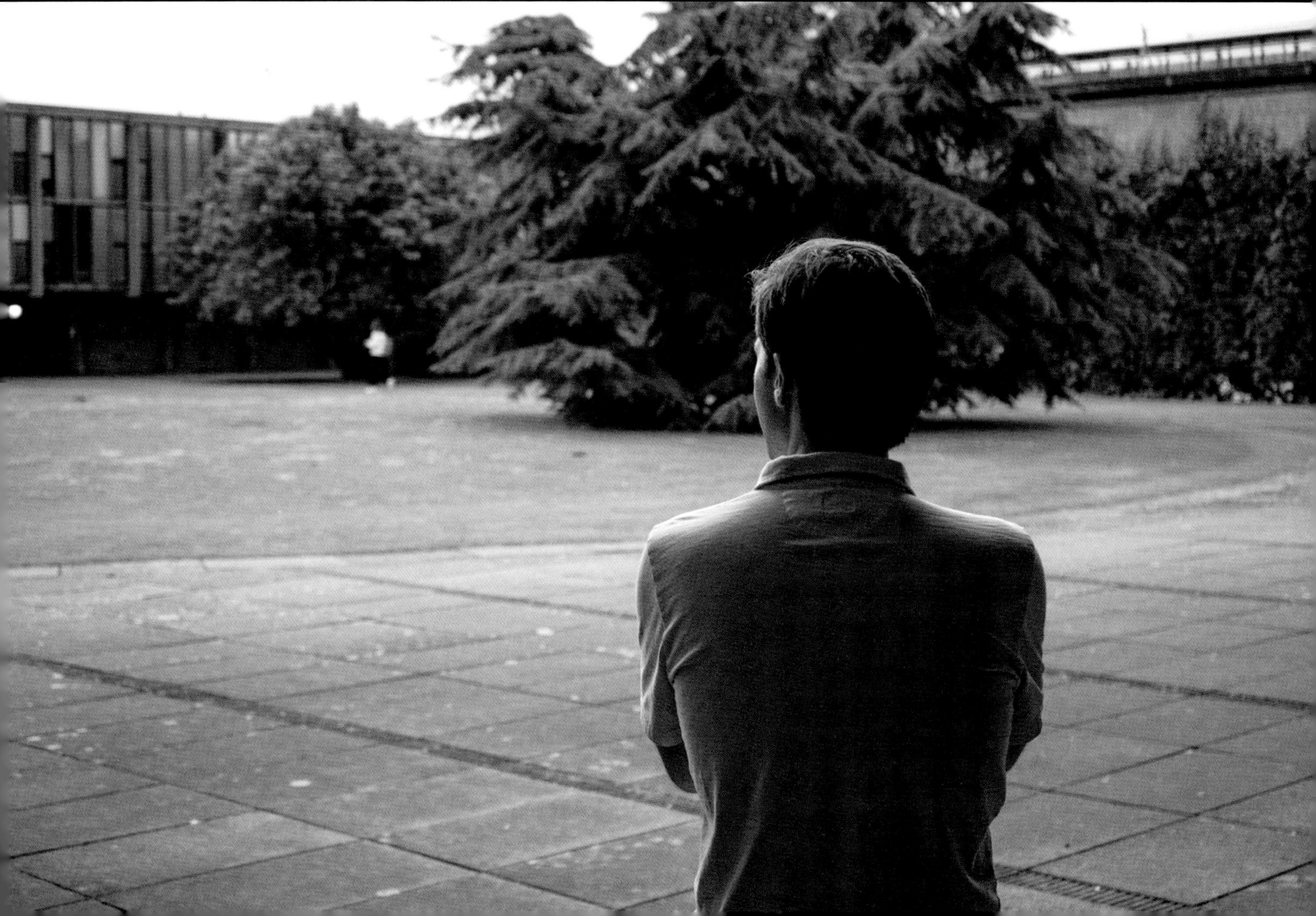

Love it or hate it

You either love Catz, or you do not. Most of the students who were interviewed clearly love the place and its history.

Ben Holden, Experimental Psychology

6
The first thing I'd like to talk about is the doorknob

What were your first impressions when you first arrived at St Catherine's?

Before I came here, during my interviews, I had seen some of the other Oxford colleges. The thing that struck me most of all was just how different Catz was compared to the other Oxford colleges. That goes without saying, obviously; this was built several hundred years after most of the other colleges were built. It just really caught me by surprise, because I didn't know anything about the college at all. I didn't know when it was built, I just knew that it existed as a college, and I was told I had an interview there. So I turned up and wasn't really expecting anything like what I saw. My first impression: I really liked how communal it was. I think because it was built a lot more recently than the other colleges, the design had the actual life of the student more in mind. A lot of the other colleges, you've got the bar, and you've got the common room. They're just completely separate places. I really liked how, at St Catherine's, it was all in the exact same place. It was just this one big area, and I think that made it seem more communal than some of the other colleges.

How does the architecture, design, or landscape affect you in your everyday life?

I think it's really open, which is something I quite like. Just because of the location as well, it's really quite quiet. It's a very relaxing place because it's got lots of open space. And it's a brilliant location because we've got the good view here, we've got these wonderful bits of green all around, we've got a really big quad. It's very greenspace. And we've got a river going by, and it's on its own little island. So that's a lovely spot. Although the downside of that was, you'd have to get someone to come in to, like, remove the sewage. So that was a downside; sometimes you've got quite a bad smell when that was happening. But generally, I thought it was a really open place and really quite relaxing because of that.

At Catz, there are six or eight rooms on a floor, which is more than at most colleges, so that's quite a good way to get people to socialise. Leaving your room, you would see someone almost immediately. I think it's really a communal place, which makes it very easy to relax and get your own time as well.

Is there a room, place, or section that is your favourite – or least favourite – location, and why?

The bar would go without saying, for the fun of it. From a design point of view, I think the SCR. I just think it's really nice, and it's very cosy, with the wood and the warm lights. And I like that where the old MCR used to be, they've got their own little walled-off gardens. So that's just a little quiet space. At the back of college next to the river, the Music House, and the Master's Garden, those are just really lovely spots. I think it's because it's lots of green, it's a relaxing place to be.

In terms of least favourites, the one bit of design I really dislike is the Master's lodgings. It's really quite ugly. It's just like this big square. A lot of the college is quite square but in an interesting way. The Library is square, but it's got grates over the windows and the little bit that juts out at the top makes it quite interesting. But the Master's lodgings look like a temporary building. It's a shame, because it's one of the first things you see when you walk in. That's the only bit I can think of that I really dislike in terms of the design.

If you had to use a metaphor for St Catherine's character, what would it be?

It's almost going to sound like a bad thing, but I don't mean that way. I almost feel like the college seems quite militaristic. It's because of all the concrete, and a lot of the non-concrete parts are either dark brown or dark green colours. It's all very uniform, with the long lines of the accommodation blocks.

Going back to the SCR, it almost feels like it could be a military headquarters. I do like that, even though it feels quite militaristic. Almost stoic in a way, very proper, almost.

Can you describe an instance prompted by Catz's physical setting, architecture, or environment that was particularly memorable for you?

In the new Quad, the windows of all the rooms have got a sheet of metal next to it. And I remember one morning, in my second-year accommodation, an early afternoon when I woke up and opened the window, the sun hit this bit of metal next to the window on the block opposite me in the perfect way. And it reflected almost directly into the room. And it looked like it was glowing. I remember thinking that was really, really cool.

Is there anything we haven't talked about that you would like to cover?

Arne is like this celebrity around here. But I think that a lot of people view him as this quite funny figure. I think just because they say he designed everything, down to the chairs, wasn't it? I think that's quite fun. There's a little sense that some of the parts of college are a little bit over-designed, in a way. And when I say some parts of the college, the only thing I'm really thinking of specifically here is the cutlery in the SCR. It's about this really weird-shaped knife and incredibly thin fork. That's just really impractical to use. It looks cool, but it's impractical to use. He did an amazing job on the chairs, though. The chairs are incredible. They're really comfortable. One of my friends works in the hall, and he was doing a breakfast reception for a group of architects that came in. After breakfast, the leader of the group stood up, ready to take the group on to show them around, and goes: 'The first thing I'd like to talk about is the doorknob.' And I find that really hilarious, like, the level to which everything has been designed. In some cases, you think maybe it didn't need that much attention? It's just this little bit of character that Catz has: love it or hate it. I think everyone agrees there's this pretty special thing about the college.

VI

Lolita Motel: Hopes and expectations

Left: Study and tutor's office of Bart van Es, professor of English.

Right: Study and tutor's office of David Womersley, professor of English.

Next spread:

Study and tutor's office of Marc Mulholland, professor of History. The books in the room reflect a lifetime of teaching.

In one of the most widely quoted reviews from 1964, architecture critic Reyner Banham compared St Catherine's College to the equally new Churchill College in Cambridge. In his review, Banham called St Catherine's 'Oxford's best motel':[198] a metaphor he repeated four times in his piece. He insisted that he meant no insult to the city, but the long rows of seemingly identical dwellings under the loggias, the cantilevered elements over the open arcades along both sides of the buildings, were the source of comparison.[199] They were reminiscent of the carport roofs over the doors of a motel with the occupant's car parked just outside. He acknowledged that the motel reference might offend those 'preoccupied, perhaps with sleazy imagery of Lolita'. In Vladimir Nabokov's novel *Lolita*, the older Humbert Humbert fell in love with the just 12-year-old Lolita and worshipped her as a goddess on a years-long journey across the United States, as they moved from motel to motel.[200]

Reading Banham's article today, the reference to *Lolita* is far more applicable than Banham even realised. It can help shed light on and decode the relations between:

1. St Catherine's new architecture and the older Oxford.

2. The building's simple geometry versus its perceived complexity.

3. Aesthetic pleasure versus architectural morality.

4. Fiction versus practice.

198) None of the articles referring to Banham's 'motel' actively use and analyse his otherwise harmless reference. See, e.g., Jackson, S. (2002). Oxford's 'Best Motel': The dining room at St Catherine's College, Oxford. *Architectural Design*, 72 (4), 22–25; St Hill, C. (2012). It is 50 years since St Catherine's, the youngest of the Oxford University colleges, was designed by Arne Jacobsen. *Blueprint* (London, England), (318), 29; Gregory, R. (2004). Teaching an old cat new tricks. *Architectural Review*, 215 (1284), 74–79.

199) Banham, R. (1964). Criticism: St Catherine's College, Oxford, Churchill College, Cambridge. *The Architectural Review*, 136 (811), 175.

200) 'Lolita, light of my life, fire of my loins. My sin, my soul. Lo-lee-ta.' Nabokov, V. (1955). *Lolita* (p. 11). Putnam.

In his epilogue to the novel, Nabokov quotes a reader for viewing the generation gap in the novel as 'Old Europe debauching young America':[201] the older person's infatuation with the young nymph. The gap between the historic college architecture in Oxford and a new build in the style of international Modernism is great, perhaps greater than assumed, which is what makes it such a perfect setting for an *Endeavour* episode revolving around 'poetical science':

> *St. Catherine's was something of a breakthrough for modern architecture in Oxford and remains a rather isolated phenomenon.*[202]

As with Lolita, you are allowed to love the nymph from a suitable distance, but you can never fall in love.

Banham viewed Jacobsen's regular distribution of the buildings on a flat, empty plot of land as an expression of strict architectural morality:

> *There can be no mistakes and no excuses, no afterthoughts and no escape-clauses, about the siting of the individual components of the scheme. No room for improvisation, no exploiting the happy accident – and no room for growth. Though the views from St. Catherine's are open, the architectural possibilities are satisfied and closed.*[203]

In a comparison of St Catherine's in Oxford and Churchill College in Cambridge, the two universities combined into the portmanteau 'Oxbridge', Michael Manser was shocked with St Catherine's strict and 'forbidding' style in yellow bricks and grey concrete, while Churchill College was seen as informal, asymmetrical, and varied – altogether more 'British'.

Each of the accommodation blocks consists of eight independent components with its own staircase.

Each block has two dwellings on the ground level and five on the upper floors with one communal bathroom, toilet, and small kitchen per staircase per floor. Thus, there are ten dwellings per house, a total of 160 per block. This layout is based on the old British college traditions.

Thanks to the floor-to-ceiling windows in the student rooms, the changing weather will always play a role in creating significant and engaging settings for studies and student life.

201) Nabokov, V. (1955). *Lolita* (p. 285). Putnam.
202) Banham, R. (1964). Criticism: St Catherine's College, Oxford, Churchill College, Cambridge. *The Architectural Review*, *136* (811), 175.
203) Ibid., 176.

The vegetation in the garden is an integrated part of daily life in the student rooms, which visually expands them.

Despite the standard furnishings, all the student rooms are individual and personal.

St. Catherine's is a relentless and unequivocal product of the machine age. It has the look of a machine, precise and exact [...] a machine for learning in.[204]

Like the best machines, it had a certain grandeur, and this was where it became architecture, honest and liberated from contemporary jargon, he argued.

In St Catherine's College, aesthetic pleasure was kept in check by moral vigilance. Or, as Humbert said, while on death row, quoting an old (fictitious) poet:

The moral sense in mortals is the duty. We have to pay on mortal sense of beauty.[205]

The bliss brought about by the aesthetic of 'Oxford's best motel' was a vital dimension of the experience, with architectural consistency the price to be paid.

Finally, the true architectural accomplishment of St Catherine's is that the experience of the place varies so widely and depends on the individual's capacity for imagination. 'Unexpected views, levels and disappearing tricks', as the architecture critic Stephen Gardiner enthusiastically wrote about Oxford's enigmatic complexities.[206] Banham's imagination gave him a sense of being a public areas of a well-designed service building of a transport facility, like an airport or, again, a motel.

One could be anywhere in North America, Scandinavia or even Australia.[207]

Had this been an actual motel, it could have been located anywhere – it depends entirely on the individual's imagination.

204) Manser, M. The Oxbridge Double. (1964, 26 July). *The Observer*.
205) Nabokov, V. (1955). *Lolita* (p. 258). Upton.
206) Gardiner, S. Changing Masterpiece. *The Observer*. (IIJ Box 9_Magazine articles).
207) Banham, R. (1964). Criticism: St Catherine's College, Oxford, Churchill College, Cambridge. *The Architectural Review*, *136* (811), 179.

Catz in a time of fundamental changes

On Matriculation Day, new students formally join the college. Led by Professor Andrew Dickinson, 300 students are walking in procession from Catz to the Sheldonian Theatre in the centre of Oxford, where the first part of the ceremony takes place.

Right: Tutor's office of Kirsten Shepherd-Barr, professor of English.

Next spread:

Full academic dress is required on Matriculation Day. This consists of a dark suit, trousers or skirt coupled with a white collared shirt or blouse, and a black tie or white bow tie as well as dark socks or black tights or stockings and black shoes.

During the 1960s, higher education underwent profound changes both socially and emotionally and in relation to gender, racial, and enrolment policies. St Catherine's College was one of the first five exclusively male colleges in Oxford to latch onto these new developments.

It is not my intention here to shift the focus to the profound changes that took place during the 1960s – the student rebellion, the peace movements, the civil rights movements, women's liberation, women's changing role on the labour market, and other fundamental transformations in the Global North – but rather to contribute relevant insights into gender policy changes at St Catherine's during this time in order to add valuable dimensions to a broader understanding of the college we see today. Unlike the changes happening in higher education in the United States, the changes in the elite universities in Cambridge and Oxford were closely related to the people leading the institutions at the time.

Both in Britain and in the United States, enrolment to elite universities changed radically from 1969 to 1974, as men and women were now admitted on equal terms and studied in co-ed settings. Universities were also beginning to accept students from families of limited means. Over a relatively short span of time, these developments led to far-reaching and fundamental changes. In the early 1960s, universities on both sides of the Atlantic were still upholding the old order, in which students did not engage in social or political debates:

> *There were no big goals, no moral commitments of consequence, no engagement in the key challenges of the time.*[208]

The considerable distance between teaching staff and students meant that the tutors were not generally aware of what was happening among the students. In autumn 1964, this resulted in growing confrontations between leadership and students in many places and in increasingly radical political rallies and events calling for societal changes, both locally and globally. Universities were met with a wide range of demands, including loosening up the rigid academic environment, increasing democracy and inclusion, reforming curriculums and examinations, ensuring women's and minorities rights to academic education and a professional career on equal terms with upper-class men, and so forth.

General assumptions about the scope of women's life in physiological, mental, and moral terms, were changing. Social responsibilities, status, and privilege came under scrutiny. In *'Keep the Damned Women Out': The Struggle for Coeducation*, an impressive study of institutional archives, history books, scientific reports, news stories, unpublished manuscripts, institutional memos, alumni magazines, and transcripts of oral recollections, Nancy Weiss Malkiel points out that the introduction of the contraceptive pill in the 1960s helped to enable new social constructions between men and women – including co-ed student accommodation.[209] Meanwhile, the establishment of new colleges with modern teaching methods and new subjects were challenging the old colleges, both in terms of popularity and when it came to funding.

---

208) Malkiel, N.W. (2016). *'Keep the damned women out': The struggle for coeducation* (p. 9). Princeton University Press.

209) Ibid., pp. 20–21.

Ladies do not take showers

A questionnaire survey in British state schools in the 1970s found that the reputation of a tough competitive environment made many female students reluctant to apply to Oxford and Cambridge. A strategic PR campaign was proposed to encourage more women to apply to Britain's two top universities.

In a comment on 24 July 1964, the otherwise open-minded Alan Bullock expressed his personal doubts about the notion of coeducation.[210] Therefore, he wanted to wait and see the outcome of the experiment at New College, which was expected to go co-ed. According to Bullock, the main challenge of founding a new college was to distinguish between what was merely a fad and what was the genuine article. Later that day, he appears to have had a change of heart. In an interview in the London-based *Daily Sketch*, he said that he would be happy to see female students at St Catherine's, 'but I just couldn't stand women dons about the place'.[211]

These changes took time. As late as in 1979, some Oxford colleges were still gender-exclusive, for example the 650-year-old Oriel College, the university's last all-male college.[212] Oriel argued that it was prudent to wait and see how things worked out at the other colleges. The proposed change was groundbreaking indeed, as this bastion of gender-segregated education since the 11th century was about to fall.

The male students welcomed coeducation, but the leadership was not necessarily of a similar mind. In 1963–1964, 16% of all university students in Oxford were female. The national ratio was 28%.[213] Women from several colleges reported about gender discrimination. For example, despite having adequate bathing facilities in college, they were denied access, since, as one dean explained, 'ladies do not take showers'.[214]

All-female colleges similarly had to be ready to accept male students, something which Oxford's five female colleges staunchly opposed.[215] They predicted that the historically all-male colleges would get the most qualified applicants, male and female, whilst they would get 'the dregs', which would result in lowering their academic standing. They also argued that since equal opportunities – both in and outside the academic world – were far from the norm, all-female colleges thus still had an important role to play.

Several Oxford colleges were interested in switching to coeducation, including St Catherine's, where two thirds of the governing bodies on 5 October 1971 voted to accept women, arguing that the benefits of coeducation outweighed the drawbacks. St Catherine's was used to change:

> *Our decision was reached above all by the desirability of making an Oxford education available on equal terms to women as well as to men.*

A week later, Alan Bullock summed up his opinion on the matter in a letter.[216] He pointed out that the issue of whether to accept women students had been debated when the college was founded. At the time, he was more focused on realising buildings and achieving parity between art and science as the first Oxford college to do so.[217] He had his hands full and was in no position to spearhead the issue of gender equity in education.

---

210) Rosenfield, R. (1964, 24 July). Field wanted. *Oxford Mail*, 3.

211) Please – no female dons. (1964, 24 July). *Daily Sketch*. (Box XL 1: *The Founding Master*).

212) Borders, W. (1979, 11 November). Another bastion falls to women: Oxford. *The New York Times*, 1, 22.

213) Malkiel, N. W. (2016). *'Keep the damned women out': The struggle for coeducation* (p. 21). Princeton University Press.

214) Borders, W. (1979, 11 November). Another bastion falls to women: Oxford. *The New York Times*, 1, 22.

215) Hicks, M. (2004). Integrating women at Oxford and Harvard, 1964–1977. In L. Ulrich (Ed.). *Gender in Harvard and Radcliffe history* (pp. 369–370, 375–379). Palgrave Macmillan.

216) Bullock, A., & Knapp, W. (1971, 12 October). The admission of women to St Catherine's. (XIID Box).

217) He added this information in an interview: Out of the air. (1964, 20 August). *The Listener*, 270.

Coeducation was adopted without drama in Oxford and Cambridge. By 1979, 21 of Oxford's 28 college were co-ed, and the remaining ones made the transformation in 2008.[218] By 2018, *The New York Times* reported that the University of Oxford had more female than male students.[219] According to data from the University and Colleges Admissions Service, in autumn 2017, Oxford had 1,070 female and 1,025 male bachelor students.

However, the paper also mentioned that the women continued to be underrepresented in the traditional male subjects of mathematics, natural science, and engineering.

Harriet Sergeant was one of the 30 women who were the first to be accepted into the all-male college in 1974:

The Venetian blinds that were installed in the new windows of the student rooms give the exterior a much more homogeneous and aesthetic expression. With different interior lighting, as in this early evening shot, each cell tells its own individual story.

218) Malkiel, N.W. (2016). *'Keep the damned women out': The struggle for coeducation* (p. 24). Princeton University Press.
219) Taylor, K., & Hartocollis, A. (2018, 27 January). Women outnumber men in Oxford's newest class: It only took 1,000 years. *The New York Times*.

The architecture was stark and the facilities basic. The dons decided concessions had to be made. They installed shower curtains and full-length mirrors on our two staircases. The male students promptly said they wanted shower curtains and full-length mirrors too.[220]

Looking back on her studies in the co-ed setting, she has no doubt that both genders benefited greatly from experiencing each other's culturally and biologically differences and similarities.

Penelope Gouk, who was also among the first women to be accepted, recalls that the female students were regarded as curiosities, with everyone knowing their names and faces within the first 24 hours. She also recalls that the women's presence had the positive effect of tempering the men's behaviour and making them more serious about their studies. She observes that there was 'considerably less heavy drinking and less totally idiotic and puerile behaviour'.[221]

Recent numbers (2022) for bachelor enrolment at Catz show that on average during the three-year period that included both the Covid-19 pandemic and Brexit (2019–2022), the college accepted 207 women (an acceptance rate of 16%) and 240 men (an acceptance rate of 15%).[222]

220) Ainsworth, R., & Howell, C. (Eds.) (2012). *St Catherine's, Oxford: A pen portrait* (p. 172). Third Millennium Publishing.

221) Frewer, L., & Gouk, P. (1974). *St Catherine's Year: Oxford 1977* (p. 21). St Catherine's College.

222) For Oxford University as a whole, the gender distribution is 55.2% women and 44.8% men. Recent national data show that women are still underrepresented in the traditional male subjects of mathematics (27.6% women), physics (21.2% women), and engineering (27.3% women). Source: public.tableau.com, Undergraduate Admissions Statistics – Counts.

Economy plus function equals style

The facade of the student rooms to the east has a similar play of light as the SAS hotel in Copenhagen.

Arne Jacobsen hated everything that might disturb his total designs. Especially when people moved into his houses, filling the windows with 'red curtains' and 'decorative candles'. This upset his design intention, so had he chosen the life of an artist, he would have had an easier time in this regard.[223] Similar disturbances occurred at St Catherine's. In July 1967, the Danish newspaper *Information* published a poem taunting his desire to control his works, even after they had been handed over to their occupants. The poem was a comment on a legal dispute with a homeowner who refused to comply with a statute that required certain colours and banned antennas and flagpoles in a new-built atrium house out of concern for aesthetic consistency.[224] The homeowner lost the case.

Just 25 days before Jacobsen's death, *Politiken* published an extensive interview with the architect, who sat down for an in-depth talk with journalist Anne Wolden-Ræthinge (pen name: Ninka).[225]

Among other topics, Jacobsen spoke candidly of his father's scepticism of his artistic abilities and of the value of architecture as an art form. In her follow-up question, Ninka caught him off guard, when she asked if it made him queasy to see one of his own houses fitted with droopy ruffled curtains, commonly known in Danish as 'butt-cheek curtains'. Jacobsen's answer reflects his lifelong experience of having to defend his curious exploration of form and his continued insistence on quality:

Not queasy – I just don't get it. But one day, one of my workmen said to me: Listen, Mr Architect, it's not nice of you to call my wife's curtains butt-cheek curtains! Then I felt bad, because he loved both his wife and her curtains. At that moment I realised I had overstepped my authority.

Better to accept droopy curtains than hurt someone else's feelings.

The curtains created an image of chaos in facades. A welcome element of disruption to break up Jacobsen's strict discipline? Or a breach of architectural consistency? In the background, the spires in Oxford's historic city centre.

223) Russell, J. (1964, 26 July). The master builder. *The Sunday Times*, 11.
224) Man må bøje sig for Jacobsen. (1966, 17 July). *Information*.
225) Ninka (1971, 28 February). Det nye kritiseres altid [The new is always criticised]. *Politiken*, 13.

Lolita Motel: Hopes and expectations

The new blinds would probably have been to Jacobsen's liking.

While construction was ongoing, this pavilion housed a temporary dining hall with a simple interior. The photograph dates from the early 1960s.

Renovation of the glass facades of the accommodation blocks

The most common criticism since the official opening of Catz to this day is the quality of the student rooms, including the erratic heating system.[226] In his memoirs, Alan Bullock explained the quality of the student accommodation as follows:

So the criticisms one can make – they're too hot, they're too noisy – well, the double glazing went, the louvres went, you can blame me for that, as I just couldn't get enough money. Moreover, I couldn't get enough money in time; because we had to settle the design, and once you've done that you can't suddenly say 'we've got a bit more money, now you can improve it'.[227]

The first 30 students moved in on Sunday 14 October 1962, in staircases 3 and 4. This was two years after the groundbreaking ceremony and two years before the college was completed.[228] At the time, there was no heating, no hot water, and no meeting places, and the only meal service was breakfast, served in a temporary pavilion.

Bullock described the situation as follows: 'The real problem at the moment is whether the freshmen of St. Catherine's College will starve or freeze to death in the first fortnight'.[229]

In 1963, one of the students, M. J. Carver, wrote in *The Wheel* about how baths and showers were unavailable until late into the semester.[230] When the showers finally worked, the toilets were found to be leaky. Catz gradually became more functional, and only the initial residents recalled the days when the hot-water system would only work every second day, and never on a Sunday.

By this time the pioneers of college residence were admirably qualified for the name 'The Dirty Thirty'.

Other students had more positive memories of inspiration from the architecture and rooms as pure poetry, with the lines painting a picture of reason, subdivision, and articulation to balance the formlessness and ecstasy of student life. The architecture offered a clean, syntactic mindset that might help the occupants make sense of things. Former English student Adam Foulds remembers the view from the floor-to-ceiling windows in his rooms:

I could sit and work and watch the rain moving across. As night darkened outside I would see my reflection in the glass resolving, getting brighter and clearer like a developing photograph.[231]

The stringency of the architecture promoted clarity of thought and ideas. The straight lines helped to contain the wilder energies of the poetry he was obsessed with.

The facades are glass from floor to ceiling with three fixed panes and two side panes that open. This makes the dwelling appear larger than it is. To the east, the resident has a view of green lawns, to the west, views of Holywell North Stream, a branch of the Thames. The windows had single glazing, which is why they were cold in winter and let in too much light and heat in summer.

As Alan Bullock self-critically recalled, the choice of glazing without sun shading was dictated by economic concerns. Bullock explained how Jacobsen predicted the drawbacks of single glazing and that he would have much preferred to see double glazing with integrated Venetian blinds rather than the jumble of curtains that the college set out with.[232]

Among Jacobsen's works during the 1960s, St Catherine's was one of the very few buildings without double glazing. In the early 1950s, he had used pairs of separate single-glazing panes mounted in a frame with blinds in between. This solution was used in the Søholm terraces in Klampenborg, the Munkegaard School, and Rødovre Town Hall, among other constructions. The simple reason for double glazing not being used at Catz was that the budget did not allow for it.

226) Ainsworth, R., & Howell, C. (Eds.) (2012). *St Catherine's, Oxford: A pen portrait* (p. 165). Third Millennium Publishing.

227) Bullock, A. (1984). *How St Catherine's College came to be founded* [A talk given to the Middle Common Room of St Catherine's College on 31 May 1984 by the Founding Master, Lord Bullock of Leafield; verbatim transcript] (pp. 1, 42). (LXIC Box: Talks by Lord Bullock and others: Oral history).

228) St Catherine's first students. (1962, 12 October). *Oxford Times*.

229) Davies, M., & Davies, D. (1997). *Creating St Catherine's College* (p. 98). St Catherine's College.

230) Archer, M. J. The New College (1963). The Wheel, 26.

231) Ainsworth, R., & Howell, C. (Eds.) (2012). *St Catherine's, Oxford: A pen portrait* (p. 185). Third Millennium Publishing.

232) IIJ Box 8_8_Correspondence about replacing single glazing.

What do you think Arne Jacobsen's reaction would be to the present proposal?

The western accommodation block after the facade renovation.

Next spread:

Spaces defined by parallel walls in ochre-coloured brick and dense yew hedges in autumnal colours. On the right, the Library building with copper cladding.

In the negotiations about the facade renovation with English Heritage (now Historic England), the Twentieth Century Society, and Docomo, the demands were clear: the slender proportions of the original window panes had to be preserved, and the blinds were to be as discreet as possible. The ability of the dark interior aluminium flashing to reduce the visual impact of the new glass panes seen from outside was considered an essential feature. In straightforward terms, it was underscored that the redesign should make a virtue of necessity by preserving the original frames and window furniture whenever possible and only replace them when necessary.[233]

In September 1998, English Heritage approved the facade renovation, considering that Jacobsen had already used horizontal slats in many places around the college, for example in the exterior of the Bernard Sunley Building and in the design of the ground level of the accommodation blocks. Initially, he had also explored the use of vertical bronze slats for the accommodation blocks, but this solution was rejected, as it was estimated to cost £120 per room – about a seventh of the total budget allocated for a student room. The engineers, Steensen & Varming, even came up with a motorised version controlled by the movement of the sun.

From the approval, it would take almost nine years before the glazing was replaced. The first obstacle was disagreement about the distribution of funding, especially with regard to the college's own share. By October 2003, this had been worked out to everyone's satisfaction, but the work was further delayed because a detailed study of the existing facades revealed a number of variations which the design would have to accommodate.

The design was revised accordingly, and in March 2004, the work could begin. The main installation was completed in August 2004, but the final completion did not happen until late 2007 due to challenges in the paint finish.

The former project architect, Peter Denney, and Teit Weylandt and Ellen Waade of Dissing+Weitling, the firm that continued Jacobsen's work and studio, were involved in the facade renovation, which was also closely supervised by Jacobsen's son, Johan. The facade renovation represented both a continuation of the existing design expression and an environmental improvement. When asked, 'What do you think Arne Jacobsen's reaction would be to the present proposal?', Jack Lankester replied, with conviction, 'I can confidently assert that he would have welcomed it'.[234]

---

233) Letter from Twentieth Century Society dated 16 October 1998. (IIJ Box 8_8_Correspondence about replacing single glazing).

234) Letter from Jack Lankester to Dr Diane Kay, English Heritage, dated 24 September 1998. (IIJ Box 8_8_Correspondence about replacing single glazing).

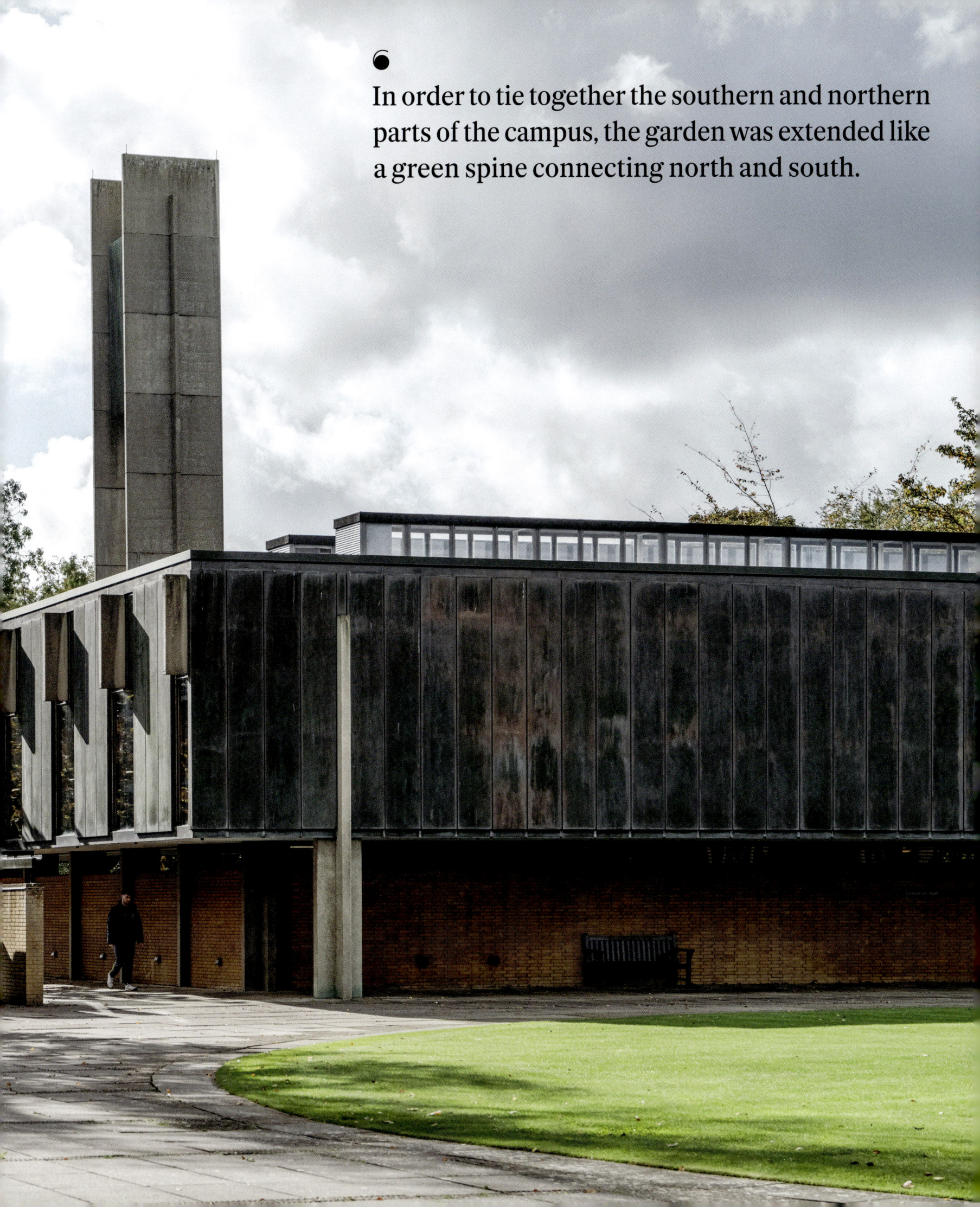

❛
In order to tie together the southern and northern parts of the campus, the garden was extended like a green spine connecting north and south.

New college buildings

Below, left: In a conversation on 10 May 2023, Knud Holscher explained that, in his opinion, the initial proposal from April 1980 was the most complete sketch and thus the one that deserved to be published.

Below, right: The new Graduate Centre at St Catherine's designed by Purcell Architects (2021). Opposite page: The extensions of the accommodation blocks to the north, designed by Hodder Associates (2005). The new main entrance with the upper horizontal framework is seen in the middle of the photo; behind it is Arne Jacobsen's Catz. See map on page 12.

Several extensions have been added to Catz: the Mary Sunley Building (1982), the Alan Bullock Building (1982), additional student accommodation by Hodder Associates (1995 and 2005), and further student accommodation and the Graduate Centre by Purcell (2021). Not surprisingly, these new builds have been situated on the previously undeveloped land to the north, and they all relate to the basic layout of Jacobsen's college and his thoughts on the direction of future expansions from 1966.

The Mary Sunley Building is a one-storey structure with a lecture theatre and meeting rooms. The purpose of the building is to enable the college to host conferences and seminars for external groups, thus providing a source of outside revenue, and to serve as 'a bridge between the college and the world outside Oxford'.[235] In connection with the Bernard Sunley Lecture Theatre – with a capacity of 240 attendants – and the Dining Hall, the new building was envisioned to allow Catz to hold conferences and seminars without disturbing daily operations. In addition, it should contain offices, toilets, and a variety of service facilities.

Knud Holscher, who by then was a professor in Denmark, and Jack Lankester served as consultants for the project. Lankester had been involved from the beginning, heading the visit to Denmark in November 1958 to visit selected architecture firms. Holscher offered three very detailed draft proposals in April 1980, followed up by alternative proposals in June and July that same year. Phase 1 included ten tutors' offices and a meeting room, totalling just over 37,500 square feet. The outlined project was situated on a very narrow plot to the north-east and had an exterior that closely matched the existing college: one storey, large window apertures, courtyard gardens, and ochre-coloured brickwork. Phase 2 was detached from this section and only contained conference facilities, totalling 37,000 square feet. It was situated on a similarly narrow plot in the north-west corner, where the Alan Bullock building now stands.

In July, these proposals were supplanted by the project that now stands on the north-eastern plot. It appears that the average 60% pay gap between Denmark and Britain also made Holscher's bid seem too dear, since the British practice did not normally involve paying for hours spent during the sketching phase, and the final fee could not amount to more than 6% of the total cost of the project. 'There are some aspects of the design which seem extravagant', as Jack Lankester observed.[236]

Lankester thus took over the detailing, but his work largely adhered to Holscher's third draft proposal.

The two men agreed that the location to the north-east provided the easiest access to the rest of college and the car park and bike shed. On 1 August 1980, the Bernard Sunley Charitable Foundation donated £200,000 to the project, provided it was named after Mary Sunley.

In the conference building, to the right of the foyer, lies the meeting room with a bar, kitchen, and offices. To the left lies the conference theatre with room for 78 attendants as well as toilets and offices. As is typical of the rest of the college, daylight and vegetation play a prominent role. The building was officially opened on 30 September 1982. It has a concrete foundation with reinforced concrete on the ground level, brick-faced cavity walls with interior blockwork cladding,

---

235) Quotation from Alan Bullock's farewell address as Master. Letter from Derek Davies to the Bernard Sunley Charitable Foundation, dated 6 October 1980. (Box IVA 2: The later buildings of the College).

236) Letter from Jack Lankester to Finance Bursar A. B. Tayler dated 14 July 1980 and a letter to Acting Master Derek Davies dated 16 July 1980. (Box IVA 2: The later buildings of the College).

prefab concrete roof members covered with asphalt, metal window frames, and interior and exterior wooden doors.

The exterior form of the Alan Bullock Building follows Knud Holscher's draft proposal from July 1980, but the floor plan is different.[237] It contains ten rooms for guest lecturers, separated by halls and courtyard gardens designed and established with respect for the existing trees. As far as I have been able to ascertain, the Alan Bullock Building was officially opened in 1983, with Jack Lankester as the architect.

The extensions by Hodder Associates (1995 and 2005) and Purcell (2021) were carried out in response to the growing student body at Catz. As mentioned earlier, it is currently the largest college at the University of Oxford, which has led to a natural demand for additional accommodation.[238] The location was not pre-determined, as the decision-makers wanted to keep an open mind to any and all possibilities. In the early 1990s, the Manchester-based architecture firm Hodder Associates was among the invited participants in the first competition for these extensions. Their proposal was a cross-shaped distribution of rooms around what was then a squash court and which now houses the fitness centre in the south-east corner. The capacity was insufficient, and the building was too close to the existing student blocks, which were listed a few years later.

In the next round of the competition, the area north of Catz was designated as the site of the coming proposals. This was also the area that Jacobsen had envisioned as the setting of future extensions. The new projects would be constructed in two stages. Phase 1, towards the north-west, followed the 17-degree angle of Holywell North Stream, while Phase 2 was planned in extension of the Master's house. At the time, it comprised three pavilions and staircases 17–19, with a total of 54 dwellings. The design used the same 9.8-foot grid that Jacobsen had used in the original student rooms, and the main material was a similar yellow brick used for the 6.5-foot-tall walls on the ground level. Phase 1 was completed in 1995 and cost about £1.4 million (about £3.37 million in today's money).[239]

When Phase 2 was initiated in 2002, Catz had grown so much that 130 students now lived off-campus. In order to tie together the southern and northern parts of the campus, the garden was extended like a green spine connecting north and south. The design sought to follow Jacobsen's intentions far more closely, ensure coherence and maintain the human scale. Since his student days, Stephen Hodder had been inspired by Scandinavian architecture and the humanisation of Modernism that Jacobsen, among others, represented. This was a version that emphasised the significance of site, context, texture, and materiality and gave equal attention to detail and the bigger picture. While Phase 1 had aimed to place the new accommodation blocks in direct continuation of the grid from the Master's house, this vision had to be abandoned due to the number of units that was required. The Hodder Associates extensions were completed in 2005.

During the summer months, conference activities had become an important source of revenue for the college. To accommodate this activity, the existing reception had to be moved from the western accommodation blocks to a clearer location by the road passing through the two areas to the Merton College sports grounds. Originally, there was a plan to place conference and lecture facilities at the north end to achieve a higher degree of 'intellectual symmetry' between north and south. However, these facilities were eliminated from the project.

In 2021, a further 78 new ensuite student dwellings and a cylindrical three-story Graduate Centre were added. When the initial sketches for this third phase were drawn in 2017, the college had a total of 954 students. Of them, 21% were living on campus, while 56% lived in rented rooms off-campus.[240] The round Graduate Centre contained multi-purpose rooms on the ground level, meeting rooms on the first floor and a very popular Middle Common Room on the second floor. This extension was designed by the Oxford branch of Purcell Architects. In form, scale, mass, and articulation, Purcell's student accommodation aligned closely with Hodder's Phase 2. The buildings contained a central corridor, a deviation from Jacobsen's and Hodder's designs that allowed for a lift and thus universal access to all student rooms. The student rooms were placed in three and a half pavilions. The latter was rotated 90 degrees and – curiously – only has windows to the north. The facade of the cylindrical building took its geometry from Jacobsen's circular bike shed and had bronze cladding.

---

237) Box IVA 10. The Alan Bullock Building.
238) This chapter is based mainly on an interview with Stephen Hodder on 21 April 2023.

239) in2013dollars.com/uk/inflation/1995?amount=1400000 (calculated 17 May 2023).

240) Purcell (2017). *Student accommodation and Graduate Centre St Catherine's College. Design and access statement* (p. 14). Purcell.

My favourite location is the pool table

Asmod Khakurel, Mathematics and Economics

When the students began to use the Junior Common Room in 1963, they found Jacobsen's perfectionism irritating. To them, it felt like 'aesthetic tyranny'. One student said to the reporter Tom Baistow of the Daily Herald: 'It took us five months to get a dartboard put up... Then another three months to add a scoreboard – then it had to be an arty one in ceramics.'

6
Being a part of this community has made me feel special and appreciated

What were your first impressions when you first arrived at St Catherine's?

Upon arriving at St Catherine's as a visiting student from a US college, I must admit that my initial impression was not great. I had high expectations, assuming that the resources and services would be of a similar calibre to what I was accustomed to in the US. However, I quickly realised that the University of Oxford and, by extension, St Catherine's had its own unique strengths and limitations.

Initially, I felt that St Catherine's was a modern college, and I felt that when it comes to Oxford colleges, people value rich history more.

The dining experience also left something to be desired, as I used to get the information that I needed to make the booking for the meal a day beforehand, and that was very tedious. Consequently, I was left feeling confused and didn't attend the Dining Hall for an entire week. As I wasn't included in the same mailing list as the freshers [first-year students], I wasn't sent important information about on-campus events.

Additionally, the course selection process was different from what I had experienced in the US. I found it challenging to navigate, because the college had to find tutors for the courses we were looking for. Before arriving at Oxford, I also didn't receive much information about tutorials and the teaching style, which made me feel unprepared.

However, as time went on, I began to adjust and appreciate the unique aspects of Oxford and St Catherine's. I realised that the initial struggles I faced helped me grow and learn, and I am now grateful for my experience at Oxford. While the transition wasn't seamless, it ultimately proved to be a valuable experience that I wouldn't trade for anything.

How does the architecture, design, or landscape affect you in your everyday life?

I grew up in Nepal, and back then, I never really paid much attention to architecture or landscape. I simply did not have the opportunity to travel and discover how they could affect your daily life. However, since I moved to the US for my studies and now to Oxford, I have come to realise how profoundly these aspects can impact your perspective and even your life philosophy. For instance, St Catherine's is a remarkably user-centric space, with a gorgeous view of the river right outside my window. I often see birds and other wildlife swimming in the river, and it brings me peace of mind, even during stressful academic periods. I believe that the architecture and landscape of Oxford, particularly in each college's unique design and setting, play a significant and critical role in shaping the college experience of Oxford students. They can have a profound impact on your state of mind and thought process.

Is there a room, place, or section that is your favourite – or least favourite – location, and why?

I would say my favourite location is the pool table of JCR. Since coming to Oxford, I've discovered the joy of playing pool. Though I had never played before, I now make a point to play as often as possible with my friends, and through the game, I've formed some great friendships. The pool room has become a social hub for me, particularly on Entz night, a special Friday evening where the room transforms into a lively party space. The atmosphere in the pool room is incredibly vibrant, and it's become one of my favourite places at St Catherine's to unwind and have fun with friends amidst the stress of academic life.

If you had to use a metaphor for St Catherine's character, what would it be?

Well, I didn't quite understand this question. I think it is because I do not know much about the details of Christian history, but I think there is a sub question right below it, right?

Can you describe an instance prompted by the physical setting, architecture, or environment of Catz that was particularly memorable for you?

During my first term at Oxford, there was a Catz dinner where I had the opportunity to dine with tutors and other members of the maths department. As I sat next to a tutor who had completed his entire academic journey at Oxford, from undergraduate to PhD, I felt amazed and grateful to be in the presence of such an intellectual individual. It was a special moment that I will always cherish. The conversation during dinner was equally stimulating, as we discussed topics such as the dependents meta theorem, the tutor's experiences with maths, and his journey at Oxford. This particular moment was a learning experience that I could not have imagined having anywhere else in the world, and it made me appreciate my time at Oxford even more.

Is there anything we haven't talked about that you would like to cover?

Initially, I had a negative impression of St Catz, but over time, my perspective has evolved significantly. After returning from Nepal during the spring break, I realised that the people and conversations here are unique and have helped me grow in ways I never imagined. The culture and traditions of St Catz are also special, particularly the daily formal dinners where you can enjoy a three-course meal at a very reasonable price. As someone from a culture where alcohol is not commonly consumed, the experience of having wine with tutors at these dinners was particularly eye-opening and has broadened my perspective. Being at Oxford has been a truly transformative experience that has made me more open to different opinions, cultures, and traditions. I am grateful for this opportunity and have found that being a part of this community has made me feel special and appreciated. Despite the initial inconveniences, I am happy to have shared this experience with you and will always cherish my time here at St Catz in Oxford.

VII

The other Catz

'Man about Catz' is an ironic commentary by Catz alumnus Ingram Wilcox on the size of the furniture and rooms.

The Catz module inspired the editors of *Catz Eye* to a creative representation of the architecture as a Rubik's Cube. The accompanying text reads: 'This cartoon has been used in the past by successive Catzeyes but we felt justified in pinching it for ours because we wanted to include something which would make us laugh. EDS.'

1
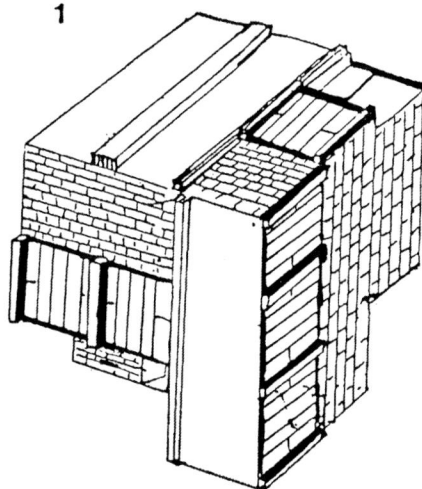

2
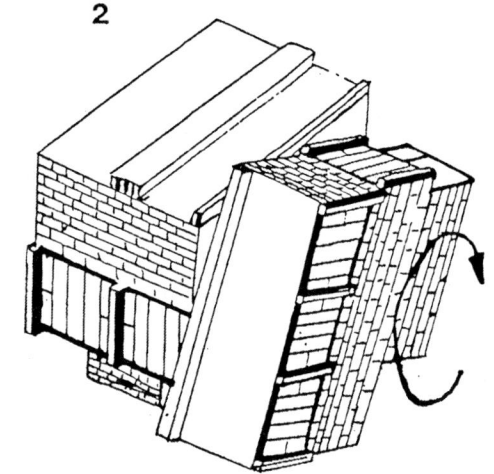

There is no doubt that, in every regard, it would have been simpler, cheaper, and less stressful to put St Catherine's students up in existing accommodation in the city,[241] but that would have undermined the Oxford tradition of small self-governing colleges. As observed by Joseph A. Soares, on-campus student accommodation is living proof that an organisational culture such as the college tradition is a vital resource in Oxford,[242] with Catz at the head of a rejuvenation process. 'The other Catz' is a story of the students who have lived here and been shaped by the architecture and the park, which over the years have aged slowly and beautifully.[243]

3

MAN ABOUT
CATZ
Ingram Wilcox

4
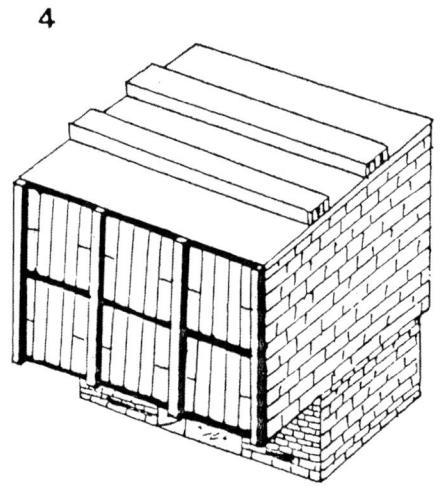

241) One of the earliest appeared in a review in 1964 by an architecture student, who was otherwise enthusiastic about the architecture. Controversial St Catherine's College considered by a student of architecture. (1964, 22 October). *The Oxford Magazine*, 29–32.

242) Soares, J. A. (1999). *The decline of privilege: The modernization of Oxford University* (p. 166). Stanford University Press.

243) Skriver, P. E. (1982). Arne Jacobsens St. Catherine's. *Arkitektur*, 2, 41.

Critical voices

For many years, Catz students published a well-edited magazine with poems, short stories, analyses, reviews, opinion pieces, interviews, and reports from associations and communities with a focus on sports, debate, literature, music, and a host of other topics. From 1937 to 1941, this publication was called *Cats*; from 1941 to 1946, *St Catherine's Wheel*; and from 1946 to 1970, *The Wheel*. The magazines offer illustrative snapshots of life in Catz and key topics for the students during these periods. As with all other art, the publications develop over the years, as advances in printing technology and illustrations offer new possibilities. They also reflect the development in 'anti' words: anti-university (A-U), anti-authoritarian, anti-militaristic, anti-apartheid, and so forth.

A review of this 30-year publication run gives the clear impression that both debates and criticism were completely unfiltered. There were no restrictions on opinions or assertions, sharp words, or intellectual skirmishes:

> *We offer unreserved apologies to all individuals (and institutions) we offend; our only defence is that we mention only those who are generally known and to be generally known is worth something – some would say everything.*[244]

Generally, there was a sense of pride in the new college – apart from the student accommodation, whose transparent exterior was described as resulting in a 'goldfish bowl type of existence'.[245]

As is the case today, the criticism was directed at the small beds and rooms, the small number of kitchens and bathrooms, the transparency and the noise:

> *When clothes are draped over the window rails as is inevitable the scene is distinctly reminiscent of a Hong Kong tenement.*[246]

The discomfort of thus being on permanent display even reached the education insert of *The Times*, which worried about all that 'fuss about what happens when young men entertain young women in their rooms'.[247]

In fairness, the dimensions and quality of the student rooms were not decided by the architects but by the specifications issued by the University Grants Commission (UGC) as a condition for co-funding the project. The university's architect, Jack Lankester, who worked closely with Jacobsen, brought this up in 1998 in a letter to English Heritage.[248] In 1961, he wrote, it was decided to postpone the construction of certain non-residential buildings, as there were no funds to complete them. Hence, financial support from the (UGC) was crucial.

The UGC offered to approve a grant for the construction of student accommodation, but since this grant was the first of its kind to the University of Oxford, the UGC was concerned how it might be viewed by other colleges in a time of rapid growth in the student population.

Thus, the grant came with the absolute requirement that student rooms could be no more than approximately 130 square feet,[249] had to adhere to the newly developed UGC formula for student rooms, and could cost no more than £840 per dwelling to establish.

These tight requirements were followed up with an ultimatum that the grant must not be supplemented by either college or university funds. Any attempts to expand the grant by adding internal funds was thus not attempted, as the money simply was not there. The cost-cutting process continued, and another £170,000 was trimmed off the budget.

Jacobsen accepted the financial limitations, but the result was student rooms that were smaller and, in every way, more spartan than originally intended. A key topic of discussion was the windows. The main concerns were the lack of privacy, discomfort from sunlight, and the transmission of noise. Heat loss was a lesser concern, as oil prices were below 2 US dollars per barrel in the early 1960s, although OPEC raised this price by 70% in 1973. The railing across the windows was required for safety reasons but was a concern for the architect, who predicted a messy appearance due to drying laundry draped across the bar. Curtains were a much cheaper solution than shades or blinds, and Jacobsen hoped in vain that they would remain closed.

---

244) Gibbons, R. E. (1961). Trinity Term, 1961. *The Wheel*, 1.
245) Bamber, R. H. (1963). Trinity Term, 1963. *The Wheel*, 1.

246) Archer, M. J. (1963). The New College. *The Wheel*, 24.
247) Behind Glass. (1964, 24 July). *The Times, Educational Supplement*.
248) Letter from Jack Lankester to Dr Diane Kay, English Heritage, dated 24 September 1998. (Box IIJ 8_8_Correspondence about replacing single glazing).

249) Skriver, P. E. (1965). St. Catherine's College i Oxford. *Arkitektur*, 1, 6.

Unimpressed

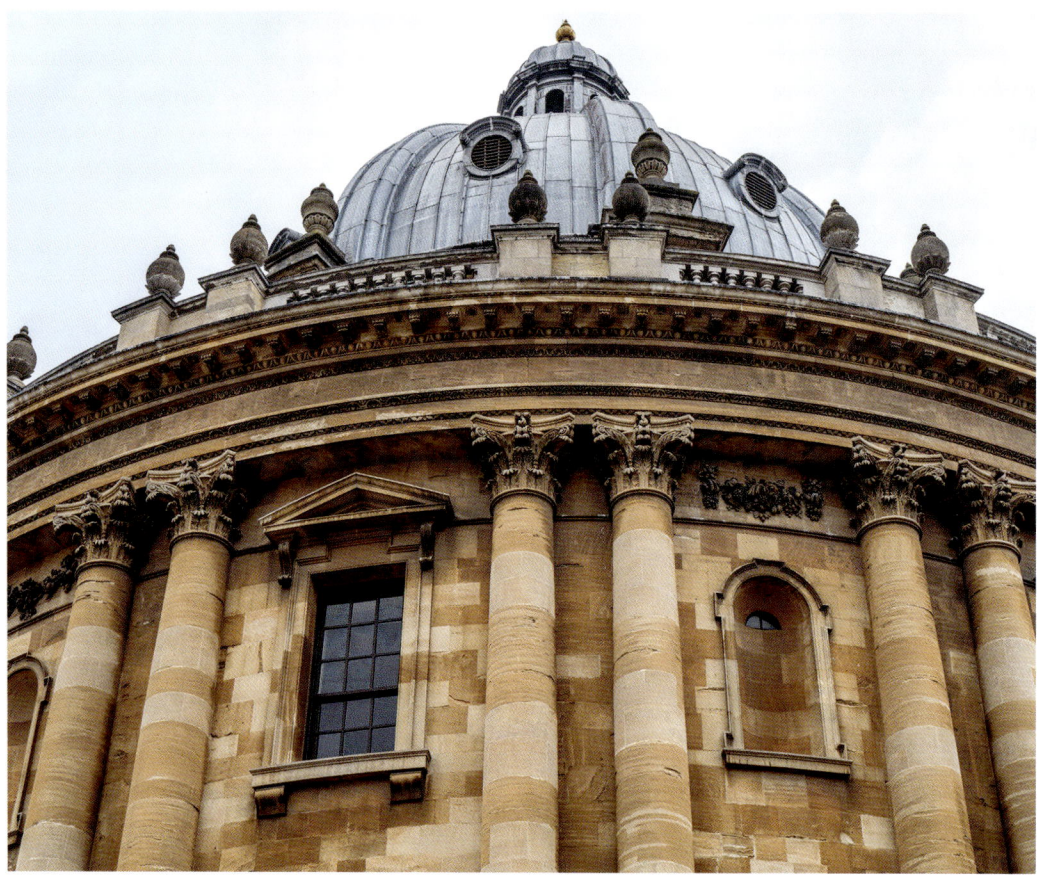

The Wheel is also where we find a dystopia of St Catherine's, with the college in ruins, as decay has taken over. This short story may be read as an apocalyptic prophecy about Catz. In his 1967 story 'Come Again', Barney Trench describes how Catz looks 40 years after the end of days, which he calls 'The Reversal'.[250] By then, what was left of the road leading up to the college had become a ditch overgrown with thorns and rusty scrap iron. Fragments of bones lay scattered around a pile of black fabric with a tassel, thrown among the nettles. All the buildings lay in ruins, and the windows had long since been broken by the impact of rain and time.

When the protagonist reached the Senior Common Room, he found 'a tomb, its ghosts of conversation echoed in the screech of rats that now swarmed over the remains of chairs'. He proceeded to what was left of the Junior Common Room, where the recessed central debate forum had been flooded. Ducks were swimming in the water. Everywhere, climbers, cactuses and vines were growing wild, forming a jungle that was spreading uncontrollably into the hall. Overhead, bats scattered.

Only the top three feet of the accommodation blocks protruded from the marshy meadow, the backs of the buildings broken. The Bernard Sunley Lecture Theatre was full of birds, like a giant aviary of birds chirping loudly in anticipation of a lecturer who would never show up. Their nests blocked the grids in front of the windows.

In the Library, water was dripping, the shelves sloping. Thousands of paper notes saying 'Return immediately' were stuck to the slimy walls, and the floors were overgrown with weeds. The protagonist discovered a black metal plaque reading 'Nova et Vetera' and walked away from the place in the afternoon dusk:

> *Magdalen's spires were still visible, towering as always, unconcerned by this ruin nearby, unchanged. Unimpressed.*

Whatever one's architectural preferences, Radcliffe Camera is one of Oxford's most famous buildings. It was designed by the Scottish architect James Gibbs and built between 1737 and 1749. The 140-foot-tall building now houses the Bodleian Library.

Oxford has made a point of marketing itself on a story about history and quality. However, as in all other British cities, it also contains the banal, clichéd, and trivial side by side with the unique.

---

250) Trench, B. (1967). Come again. *The Wheel*, 37–38.

A Certain Logic of Expectations

In his 2021 book *A Certain Logic of Expectations*, the Mexican photographer and writer Arturo Soto showcases what might be called 'the other Oxford'.[251] His book is mentioned here because Soto lived in Catz as a student, and his book aims to show the other side of Oxford, demonstrating that the city is, spatially and socially, much more than (neo-)Gothic and (neo-)Elizabethan colleges, churches, museums, and theatres, and that it also contains numerous locations bereft of architectural idealism.

Whether he turns his lens on backyards, endless rows of signs, traces of former buildings or building sections, dilapidated and broken murals, tents abandoned by homeless people, or temporary chalk lines on the asphalt, he portrays the periphery of Oxford as a large palimpsest with surfaces showing glimpses of many partially erased stories. These are vague, nameless areas that show traces of human life,[252] despite the complete absence of people in his pictures, which may be partially due to the fact that the book was created during the pandemics of loneliness: Brexit and Covid-19.

His motivation for the critique is that articles and other forms of literature about the college are full of praise. Soto remembers it differently:

As admirable as Arne Jacobsen's gifts as an architect are, many aspects of Catz are less than ideal. [...] Students develop back problems because of the narrow built-in beds – the undergrads call them straitjacket beds – that are part of his original design. The rooms get unbearably hot over the summer, and you must be prepared to deal with an army of mosquitos if you dare open the window. Or how about the beautifully designed lamps on the hall's tables that turn conversations with people sitting opposite you into a game of 'hide and seek'? There are too many flaws to report here, yet the building is always commended by architectural critics, probably because they never lived here.[253]

He supplements his own experience with contributions from others:

A friend who works as a tour guide once had an architect in a group who believed the Radcliffe Camera was the ugliest building he had ever seen. My friend then showed him a picture of Catz, which he thinks is the most unpleasant in Oxford because it looks like a swimming pool. The architect replied in amazement that he loved it and wanted to check it out.[254]

As Soto is both camera and pen in the book, the opening sentence reads:

Images come with a promise; words with a compromise. The rewards of both lie in the affinities they create, as long as we distinguish reality from reality.[255]

The recollections in the book are quick snapshots, like the photographs but less exhaustive. Oxford has been very successful in selling its historic image but less successful in selling its contemporary and everyday qualities. Hence, Catz's architecture and landscaping are like stepchildren that struggle to find their place in Soto's narrative.

---

251) Soto, A. (2021). *A certain logic of expectations*. The Eriskay Connection.

252) Ørskov, W. (1987). *Den åbne skulptur* (pp. 96–106). Borgen.

253) Soto, A. (2021). *A certain logic of expectations* (p. 41). The Eriskay Connection.

254) Ibid., p. 107.

255) 'As my friend Matías once said while having beers on the lawn of St Catherine's College (Catz)'. In Soto, A. (2021). *A certain logic of expectations* (p. 6). The Eriskay Connection.

Blisters and broken fingernails

Perspective and elevations of student room.

Anders Bodelsen could not resist commenting on the total design of St Catherine's, which students saw as difficult to use:

Naturally, there are objections. Something about closets that Arne Jacobsen wanted to hide inside the walls, which is why he has not given them handles, and as a result, people at St Catherine's go around with broken fingernails. And something about sinks, where the soap keeps slipping into the futuristically shaped bowl. And finally, there are people who go around showing the blisters they have developed trying to eat using Arne Jacobsen's cutlery. [256]

Bodelsen dismissed the complaints, arguing that beauty trumps practicality:

Functionalism is many things, and for its 50 million, Oxford gets more than a college that largely promises to be more utilitarian. [Oxford] also gets a work of art, a challenge and a model to continue to strive towards.

Paradoxically, it was this same beauty of the total work that caused two of England's sharpest architecture critics, Jennifer Sherwood and Nikolaus Pevsner first to exclaim, 'Here is a perfect piece of architecture', and then to see the perfection of the spaces as the project's Achilles heel.[257] As an example, they pointed to the furniture in the Junior Common Room, which was placed with such exacting geometric perfection that nothing could be moved. In their sweeping criticism, they concluded, '*C'est magnifique, mais ce n'est pas un collège*' – 'it is beautiful, but it is no college'. They argued that if a college was a college due to moods produced by different styles, sizes, forms, and outlooks, then St Catherine's was not a college; however, if a work of architecture with such a distinct, individual personality proved to be a suitable setting for young people's lives during their most formative years, this was indeed a college. Time would have to tell.

Thirty years earlier, the self-same Pevsner had opened his principal work *An Outline of European Architecture* with the words: 'A bicycle shed is a building; Lincoln Cathedral is a piece of architecture.'[258] We had to get to 1964 before the bike shed at Catz disproved that assertion.

256) Bodelsen, A. (1963, 18 July). Jacobsen i Oxford. *Berlingske Aftenavis*, 4.

257) Sherwood, J., & Pevsner, N. (1974). *Buildings of England: Oxfordshire* (pp. 243–244). Penguin.

258) Pevsner, N. (1943). *An outline of European architecture* (p. 15). Penguin.

More nonsense

John Charalambos Simopoulos – dean, philosopher, and lecturer for 60 years – was a passionate critic of Arne Jacobsen's project. There was one story in particular that he enjoyed telling about himself and his role at Catz.²⁵⁹⁾ Simopoulos felt that the paternal aspects of his work were as important as the educational, so he would visit his new philosophy students on their first evening in college to see how they were settling in. Late one evening in 1973, he knocked on a new student's door and found him sitting, stunned, on the one large piece of furniture in the room, a boxy plywood divan. Where, asked young Peter Mandelson, was he expected to sleep? With something of a gleam in his eye, Simopoulos bent down and pulled out the bed concealed beneath.²⁶⁰⁾

The distrust between the architects and Simopoulos went both ways, as the dean had many requirements for the design of his own rooms, which often conflicted with the greater whole. In a handwritten letter dated 15 August 1962 to Arne Jacobsen, Knud Holscher wrote from Catz, slightly perturbed:

*Now, Simopoulos wants glass in his windows that acts as a mirror seen from outside and glass seen from inside – I told him that this has to be run by you – as I do not have the mandate to add mirrors to your facades. This same, slightly confused person is now having a special kitchen and bathroom made and is also requesting a garage door that opens automatically… all rather childish.*²⁶¹⁾

Thirty-one years later, when the college had been Grade 1 listed, the war of words had not abated.²⁶²⁾ *The Guardian* interviewed both Bullock and Simopoulos, and while the former was delighted by the honour, Simopoulos remained unyielding. He sided entirely with the students in a sneering comment about their rooms being much too small, hot, and lacking in noise insulation:

You can't blow your nose without knocking someone off his chair next door.

To Simopoulos, the only good things were the students, of course, and the gardens; the latter because they were designed by a colleague, Barrie Juniper – they were 'the saving grace' of the place.

He admitted having been a member of staff during St Catherine's search for an architect but did not feel that he had been consulted, which is why the committee came back with this 'miserable Dane', who did not listen to his clients. He described him as gloomy as hell, a symphony by the Finnish composer Sibelius brought – more or less – to life.

*Everyone licked Alan's arse at the time. He was very impressed by Jacobsen, even let him design the ghastly cutlery you eat off in hall. When Alan showed the fellows the new knives and forks, they 'oohed' and 'aahed'; I said I thought they looked like a DIY abortion kit designed by Charles Addams.*²⁶³⁾

English Heritage explained that the listing had nothing to do with good or bad taste but was about identifying and protecting buildings of great historic and architectural significance, whether they were fashionable or not: 'Fashion is by its nature fickle.' To this, John Simopoulos curtly replied, 'More nonsense.'

---

259) *St Catherine's College, Oxford: The Year 2015* (p. 56). St Catherine's College.

260) Peter Mandelson went on to become First Secretary of State in Gordon Brown's Labour Government, followed by other senior government posts, and made Baron Mandelson in 2008.

261) Danish National Archives (Business Archive). 23 archive boxes (05591): Correspondence and more with Holscher 1962, 1966 (286).

262) 'So what if it's ugly and uncomfortable – it's important'. (1993, 7 April). *The Independent*.

263) The Arne Jacobsen cutlery was designed for the SAS Royal Hotel in 1957 for Anton Michelsen Stainless. Addams is an American artist who is known, among other things, for his black sense of humour, morbid cartoons, and the sophisticated but creepy comic series *The Addams Family*.

Catz Eye

When cockroaches were found in Catz, the editors of *Catz Eye* designed this cockroach motel, so the readers could provide the vermin with a roof over their heads.

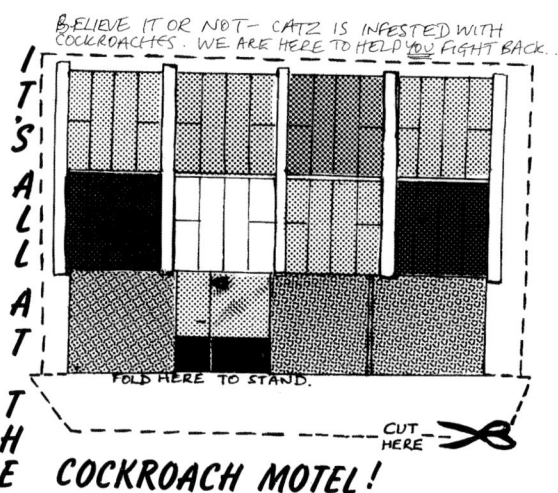

The students at St Catherine's College had their own magazine, *Catz Eye*. Like its predecessor, *The Wheel*, it featured brief reports from selected sporting events and the literary scene but in a much more risqué and provocative style. This is 110% a student's magazine, which plays creatively with the title *Catz Eye*: Ratz Eye, Hack's Eye, Patz Eye, Starcatz, and Cazzo, the latter being vulgar Italian slang.[264]

The fresh and original tone was provoking to many. So many, in fact, that in December 1978, the editors ironically acknowledged the readers' sensitivity and liberally handed out apologies, including to the Queen, the government, the miners, Mrs Thatcher, the Pope, young mothers, the Kremlin, Tarzan, political science graduates, writers, and a host of well-known and lesser-known figures.[265] The complaints that the magazine received showed that many felt 'disturbed, disgusted or righteously indignant at the content'.[266] The more bizarre the style, the better.

Arne Jacobsen and St Catherine's were fair game, too. In the 1985 edition, the essay 'Home?', written in a curious, occasionally eccentric tone, offered a snapshot of what young people thought of life in the college during the mid-1980s. Addressed to the new freshers, it made a point to introduce both places and people.

The essayist remained anonymous. Below, the first three paragraphs, which include a critical look at the student accommodation:

HOME?

This edifice of yellow brick and glass was the brainchild of the sublime yet ridiculous architect Arne Jacobsen, of Danish origin and quite obviously of Danish sense; for, let it be said, this college is the only college probably in the world that was built on an ex-rubbish tip, and it is thus prone to subsidence. In years to come tourists, more accustomed to the mullioned windows and gruesome gargoyles of Central Oxford, will flock chez nous and take pictures of the infamous leaning belltower of Catz and will marvel as, Venice-like, she sinks into the realms of Hades.

[...] All the rooms are small but some are smaller than others; and to the smallest of them all are the 1st years assigned, because it is a truth (and here I quote the great Thomas A Kempis) *THAT 'He who learneth longer groweth in Body and Spirit' so naturally it follows that the small rooms are not big enough for the second and third years* (though a certain third year mathematician I know has been allocated a cupboard for his 3rd year sojourn.) *Strangely, as you enter your room, you are met by a second white door whose superfluity is legend in the corridors of Catz.*

Beyond this mysterious door is a room of gargantuan (cf. 'Catzspeak' vol. 3 p. 574) *proportions, with furniture which would have done Ignatius Loyola proud. What with the window that rattleth profoundly when the wind rises above 1 knot, you would be forgiven for having the opinion of one Neil C.H. Urch, who described the rooms as resembling an asylum for voyeuristic Trappist monks.*

---

264) Italian slang, equivalent of 'prick', 'fuck', and so forth.

265) (1978, 5 December). Catz Eye. *Catz Eye Extra* (14). (Box XIIID: Catz Eye, 1978–).

266) Letter to Dafydd Rees, President Junior Common Room, 12 March 1987. (Box XIIID: Catz Eye, 1978–).

"… liberally handed out apologies, including to the Queen, the government, the miners, Mrs Thatcher, the Pope, young mothers, the Kremlin, Tarzan…

Catz moments / Matteo Flaviocatilo, student of English and Literature

Carrying a bit of Catz home

Florence Baker Masters, Human Sciences

Florence with the dogs
Pippi and Catherine.

6
I feel like I am going to fall off!

What were your first impressions when you first arrived at St Catherine's?

That it was really open and different from other colleges. I didn't get to look at Catz before I applied here because it was Covid-19 lockdown, so all I had seen was pictures on the internet. But I really liked the windows in the rooms. You open your bedroom for the first time, and you just see loads of light. I thought that was really nice. I did come and visit it before I started, just because I was in Oxford. I remember walking around, and it just felt really open and quite calm. It feels very quiet and peaceful.

And in your first week of term, you spend loads of time in the hall. I really liked the hall; that's where I met a lot of friends because we'd all go and get food together in there. You have a lot of formal dinners in the hall. It's really big. It's very grand. What I notice more when I go to my friends in different colleges, is that a lot of other colleges feel really secretive – there's loads of secret doors and no signs telling you where to go. You just have to know where the doors and paths are, whereas at Catz it felt like you could be anyone and just know where to go (because of the simple layout).

I think as well that ties into me coming from Manchester. I come from a bit more of a normal background, compared to some of the people who went to really posh private schools that already look like Oxford. My own school looked horrible. So it's nice to come somewhere that just felt very accessible.

How does the architecture, design, or landscape affect you in your everyday life?

The windows really affect my life. I got really good at sleeping in the daytime because I was so used to sleeping with light around me, because the blinds don't work very well. That's just a very practical aspect. I notice when I go home, I have to leave my blinds open in my room. Otherwise I can't sleep because it's too dark, so it's like carrying a bit of Catz home with me.

What else? I think I really ended up not liking the room so much at the end of my first year, just because they get really warm in summer. And you're constantly thinking about work, and because the bed is tucked up on a shelf, it never feels very relaxing. I do really like the furniture here, though; it's actually really posh furniture. It always makes me laugh. Because most student accommodation isn't very nice, so to have these chairs that people desire, it makes me smile.

Is there a room, place, or section that is your favourite – or least favourite – location, and why?

I really liked the walk from the JCR down towards Old Quad. I used to live on the furthest away staircase and have to walk down there every day. And that was just so nice because it is that same view every time you're going back to your room, it's quite a nice walk. It felt really peaceful, because all the lights are glowing in it at right angles. Every time I'd walk through there, it has the same impact, like, 'oh, wow, that looks really cool'. I think, in Oxford, you can get really used to the architecture. It's like 'oh, look at this beautiful building on a street of beautiful buildings'. Whereas that was definitely a view that felt fresh every time I saw it.

If you had to use a metaphor for St Catherine's character, what would it be?

I was trying to think about this, and I couldn't think of one. I don't know if I'd have a metaphor, but I do have a way to describe it. I just think it feels very open and very peaceful. It always feels like a lot of Oxford's just in your face. A lot of Oxford architecture is very, very pretty, but it's incredibly detailed. Catz is just a bit cleaner. It's not adding any stress in my life. Some other colleges feel really claustrophobic, whereas I think Catz is really flat as well. It always feels very calm. It's just fit for purpose.

Can you describe an instance prompted by the physical setting, architecture, or environment of Catz that was particularly memorable to you?

I have really nice memories of revising on a bit of grass behind the old quad. Me and my friend would go there and put a blanket down and just sit in the sun. We would really appreciate that little quiet area. A way to get out of your room and just sit down. But that's a really fun memory, sitting with her, revising and just feeling really calm because of all the plants around you.

Is there anything we haven't talked about that you would like to cover?

I really hate the kitchens. But I don't know if they're original. I guess Catz was built without thinking of people who might want to use the kitchen. All the kitchens are just slotted into corridors like tiny rooms. I really don't like it because I don't want to have to pay for food in hall, but I also can't really cook in this corridor for 10 people, so I really hate the kitchens! But I think that's my only grievance. Oh! And the stairs in the Library. I really don't understand them, because they feel really scary. The barriers are so thin and I feel like I am going to fall off!

VIII

The most Oxford of Oxford colleges

The Junior Common Room, the Quad, and the Dining Hall are among the most popular locations in Catz, because they promote the social encounters that are one of the intrinsic qualities of the college.

Next spread:

The ever-changing west facade with the former main entrance. Like a work by the Dutch artist Piet Mondrian, whose stringent compositions of vertical and horizontal lines filled in with colour blocks had a significant impact on architecture, including in constructivism.

'What sort of a place is it?' asked R. H. Bamber, the editor of *The Wheel* in 1963, when the first buildings had been completed.[267] Or, even more importantly, what sort of personality is it that is going to emerge in the future? Although Catz was planned around a full-blooded Oxford image…

> *St. Catherine may become the most 'Oxford' of Oxford colleges. It is to be hoped that St. Cath's will not become just another Oxford college, but will always have something unique to offer.*

The new-born college was met with high expectations, since 'the life of a college will not be the life of a child but that of many children'.[268] As early as in 1963, the students announced that Catz was free and self-governing because it came naked into this world. It was free to rethink all the old traditions and practices without being obligated to embrace any of them. Unburdened by heritage, the college could freely absorb and modify the traditions that proved useful. And discard the ones that were obsolete. In a constant endeavour to be contemporary – present in the moment. So how did it go?

This book offers some of the answers. As the many voices from the past and present illustrate, there are many opinions about what sort of place Catz has become. There are those who love the place. Those who think it is a good place to work but not to live. And those who do not like it.[269] Regardless of these assessments, Catz stands out in three regards: innovative architecture, social diversity, and social awareness.

Alan Bullock's comment that 'the influence of buildings on people is not properly understood' is correct. We lack insight, but as we can see from the interviews, among other sources, architecture does play a prominent role. Students choose Catz because of its architectural and natural qualities and soothing effect (Biba Jones and Jake McMillan). They appreciate it and find that it brings people together who have a special (social) character and contributes to a special, shared identity (Mia Campbell). Even when the buildings seem reminiscent of 'a military headquarters' (Ben Holden), this is not a negative assessment. They are stoic in their simple layout (Florence Baker Masters), and motivating even on a bad day (Jake McMillan). There are many who do not like the student rooms, and there are those who love them (Martin Alfonsin Larsen). By being innovative and 'the cooler younger sibling' (Kelsey Moriarty), Catz – paradoxically – preserves all the qualities of the old institutions, since they all have an undying admiration for their architect.

The democratic layout of the architecture defies the expectations of an elite Oxford enclave – the reserve of the few (Asmod Khakurel). At a social level, places and activities encourage interaction and attract young people (Mia Campbell). In both the Junior Common Room and the new Middle Common Room, social activities are intertwined with cultural and academic ones. On this topic, the statements show that the common rooms, the Dining Hall, and the outdoor spaces foster and cultivate friendships (Martin Alfonsin Larsen) and favour spontaneous encounters through the accessibility of the architecture. Also, it does not hurt that the bar in the Junior Common Room is famous throughout Oxford as the best and cheapest meeting place.

---

267) Bamber, R.H. (1963). Trinity Term, 1963. *The Wheel*, 1.

268) Macdonald, K. (1963). The birth of a college. *The Wheel*, 28–29.

269) Webb, M. (1966, 17 February). A jewel amid the dreaming spires. *Country Life*, 350.

The RAAC (Reinforced Autoclaved Aerated Concrete) elements were simple to install here in the student accommodation of Catz in the early 1960s.

Right: Project architect Peter Denney in 1964 in the self-same student accommodation. During the 1960s and 1970s, these lightweight concrete elements were widely used all over the world.

Epilogue | Back to the future

Bullock wanted a 'classless society' in his college, and he – almost – achieved it: 'I'm very much aware how much class bothers people.'[270] In terms of class, Catz continues to aim for the finest minds, regardless of social status. Catz still has the ambition of an equal distribution between science and the humanities, but this has not yet been achieved, in part because women are less likely than men to apply to mathematics, engineering, and similar fields.

Catz, Oxford's youngest college, is spearheading a rejuvenation process with a national impact in architecture, ethics, and economics. It would be erroneous and imprecise to say that Oxford's and Cambridge's other colleges are not also contributing to this effort, each in their way. They are, in a wide range of areas, including a strong economy, aristocratic architecture, and deeply rooted traditions. All Oxford colleges have an easier time fundraising than other British colleges. They can all, rightly, take pride in sublime architecture and centuries-old traditions, but Catz will always be aware that with its radical architecture, it is pushing boundaries – in architectural history and in our minds.

In September 2023, the British authorities closed down more than 100 learning environments all over the countries due to safety problems with RAAC. In a damp climate, the rebars rust and may collapse without warning. During the 1950s and 1960s, RAAC was widely used in floors, walls, and ceilings because it was cheap and easy to install. In 2023, Catz was forced to close down the college's administration, Library, kitchen, Dining Hall, lecture theatre, Junior Common Room, and Senior Common Room as well as the top-floor student rooms. Freshmen had to study and sleep in tents and share bedrooms. On page 175, there is a photo of the temporary dining hall around 1963. Sixty years later, new temporary pavilions are popping up: back to the future.

270) Manuscript for article by Tom Baistow. (Box IIJ Complete, Box 9_The Architect-Press cuttings_6).

The most Oxford of Oxford colleges

Catz moments / Dame Shalini Amerasinghe Ganendra. Associate Academic in the Department of Art History, Oxford University

My neighbour's room is a sanctuary

Jake McMillan, Philosophy, Politics, and Economics (PPE)

Grazing sheep are a rare sight. Even though Catz is located on the outskirts of Oxford's historic city centre, it is still an urban setting.

6
It is like taking a deep breath.

What were your first impressions when you first arrived at St Catherine's?

I felt very calm. I thought that my windows and my room were nice and pretty. And I just think the layout of the whole place made me feel really calm when I arrived. I was quite anxious on my first day here, but, yeah, the layout was calming.

How does the architecture, design, or landscape affect you in your everyday life?

My windows are probably a blessing and a curse – the blinds let in quite a lot of light, which means I wake up to natural light every day. It's great, sometimes a bit early, but I get to look out onto the green fields. So that is really inspiring. I feel more motivated to do things, even on a miserable day. Also, I spent quite a lot of time in the JCR. It's a very open room, easy to socialise in, and I just think it's a very good place to be. Perhaps the only negative in my daily life is the kitchens – they are too small. I can't think of anything else.

Is there a room, place, or section that is your favourite – or least favourite – location, and why?

My favourite place is actually my neighbour's room. He's got a slightly bigger one, but he's made it into a real sanctuary. It's really well laid out, and I spend a lot of time in there talking to him and our friends. I feel very comfortable in that room. And the bar is really good. I bring a lot of friends over there. I think it's a great place to unwind. My least favourite location is probably the kitchen, just because I like to cook and it's not very well equipped. The bathrooms are fine, but a lot of my friends in other colleges have ensuites. I get a little bit jealous, going and seeing them.

If you had to use a metaphor for St Catherine's character, what would it be?

The word 'sunrise' comes to mind. I just think it's a very bright and important place. And like I said, I'm always looking out onto the green. It feels very light and sunny, even when it's not. Yeah, the word 'sunrise' comes to mind.

Can you describe an instance prompted by the physical setting, architecture, or environment of Catz that was particularly memorable to you?

I guess it's more like an ongoing thing: the arch made by the overhanging rooms in the old quad is incredible. It makes a perfect right angle all the way down the staircases that is really beautiful. Every time I walk down there, I feel very grounded. It is like taking a deep breath. Also, in winter, when you walk around, you can see all of the bedrooms from the quad lit up. In each one, there are unrelated people doing their own things. In a way, you feel disconnected, but it is also nice to see all these candid events and see it all happen. It feels well designed for a university.

Is there anything we haven't talked about that you would like to cover?

I think we're very lucky to have a lot of facilities, like a gym. We've got food three times a day, and it's good food on the go, we are very lucky to have that. And in comparison to accommodations around the country, we are lucky. My girlfriend's at UCL [University College London], and her room is really cosy, but it is in a basement and only gets a square of natural light on her wall every day. Whenever she comes to visit, she is in awe about accommodation here.

Archival materials

Illustrations

Literature

TV and film

Index

About the author
and the photographer

Acknowledgements

Archival materials

PRIMARY ARCHIVE BOXES AT ST CATHERINE'S COLLEGE:

PHOTOS, DRAWINGS, AND RELEVANT WRITTEN SOURCES

II The Creation of the College

J The architect

BOX 1: Choice of architect

Press cuttings on appointment of Jacobsen as architect

'On being a client' by Alan Bullock – Notes on Oxford Colleges

Correspondence on choice of architect, 1958

Correspondence on choice of architect, 1959

Correspondence with Jacobsen and his staff, 1959–1969

Lord Bullock

BOX 2: Aerial views of College

Photographs – the model

Photographs – aerial view

Photographs 1990s – aerial view of College accessed 16 April 2018 from James Bennet

Photographs – Holywell Great Meadow – The site

The site – October 1961

BOX 3: Photographs of the building under construction

Hall – SCR – JCR

Library

Offices – Music House – Shed

Residential blocks

Bernard Sunley building

BOX 4: Photographs of the exterior

Photographer on reverse – various photographers

Late 1960s

Early photos – Surveyor

Unidentified + 20 microfilms

AJ

Postcards

Various b/w photographs taken by Eric de Maré

Eric de Maré negatives + various photos

Founding Fellow 1959–1995

Correspondence between Eric de Maré and Lankester, University Surveyor, 1964

Architectural details – Exterior

Architectural Prospects

Early photos – 4000 series

Early photos – 100 series

BOX 5: Photos of interior details and individual buildings

St Catz interior pictures b/w

Pre-1993 Porter's Lodge

Furniture

Photographs – interiors, architectural details, 1960s

Temporary dining hut

Interiors 2000

Photographs – Junior Common Room

Photographs – Governing Body Room

Hall

BOX 6: Photographs of individual buildings

Photographs – Senior Common Room, Music House

Bell Tower

Bernard Sunley building

Music House

Library

Master's House

BOX 7: Oversize photographs

Exterior – oversize

Merton's field

Interior – oversize

Furniture – oversize

The site – oversize

Residential blocks – oversize

BOX 8: Books on Arne Jacobsen

Loose magazines

Photographs of Arne Jacobsen

Tobias Jacobsen Interview, 2011

Exhibition

Letters between Mrs Arne Jacobsen and Alan Bullock

Various: copy of the draft of the appointment letter, copy of the model etc.

How to be modern exhibition 2002, leaflets and correspondence

Correspondence about replacing single glazing in residential units with double glazing with integral blinds

Magazine articles

BOX 9: Press cuttings

Press cuttings

Special press cuttings

More press cuttings

More press cuttings

Colour slides – Photographs – Press cuttings – Negatives

More press cuttings

BOX 10: Press cuttings

Miscellaneous press cuttings

The Architect's Journal

AMC – Article by Jean Michel Leger

Magazines

SECONDARY ARCHIVE BOXES AT ST CATHERINE'S COLLEGE:

PHOTOS, DRAWINGS, AND RELEVANT WRITTEN SOURCES

IIC BOX 6

Villa Serbelloni, owned by the Rockefeller Foundation, Italy, 1961 (1)

IID BOXES 1–6

Financial planning and funding (6)

IIIF BOX 1

Materials concerning particular buildings: Master's House, Library, Music House, Bell Tower

IIIF BOX 2

Materials concerning particular buildings: Fellows' rooms, Bicycle shed, Squash court, Punt House, Kitchen, Lodge

IVA BOXES 1–4

The later buildings of the College

IVA BOX 10

The Alan Bullock Building

IVB BOX

The Workshop

IVC BOX

The Hodder Buildings, Phases 1 and 2 (1)

Illustrations

LXIC BOX

Talks by Lord Bullock and others. Oral history (1)

XIID BOKS

Closure at night (1)

XL BOX 1

The Founding Master (1)

XL BOX 10

The Founding Master (1)

VIA BOX

The College gardens (1)

VIB BOX 1

Early plans and correspondence about planning and planting the garden (1)

VIB BOX 2

Correspondence about planning and planting the garden (1)

VIC BOX

Trees in the Quadrangle (1)

VIE BOX

'Reminiscences' of Garden Master (B. E. J.)

VIIIA

Chaplaincy and religious matters

XE AND XF

St Catherine's Chronicle, 1962–1974, *The Year*, 1975–1976

XIIIC

Students' publications *Cats*, 1937–1941, 1941–1946

St Catherine's Wheel, *The Wheel* 1946–1970

XIIID

Catz Eye, 1978

DRAWING AND BUSINESS ARCHIVES

St Catherine's College: Drawing Index Complete.

Royal Danish Library, the Art Library, Søborg Study Hall: five portfolios with drawings (760) that were produced in Denmark, containing perspective drawings with watercolour wash, photos, plans, sections, and elevations as well as many details of interiors and furniture.

Royal Institute of British Architects (RIBA), British Architectural Library, Drawings & Archives Collections: three portfolios, of which portfolio 1 contains 104 drawings and sketches, portfolio 2 more than 100 drawings of a sports ground, furniture, blinds and so forth, while portfolio 3 has about 60–70 drawings of lamps produced by Louis Poulsen as well as sketches and details. Original drawings that were produced in England.

Danish National Archives (Business Archive). 23 archival boxes (05591): correspondence and minutes of meetings (280, 281, 282, 283, 284, 285), correspondence etc. with Holscher 1962, 1966 (286), architectural drawings blocks A (291), B and C (287, 292), D (288), F1 and F2 (289), J, K, L and S (190), E, J, K, L, T (299), miscellaneous drawings (301), drawings related to Louis Poulsen (302).

All the photographs in the book were taken by Rasmus Hjortshøj, except for the following:

8: Library, St Catherine's College | 12: Map, Søren Varming, Punktum Design | 16: Kemsley House, London | 20: Library, St Catherine's College | 22: Royal Danish Library, the Art Library | 25 (all): Sam Lambert | 26: Library, St Catherine's College; Wilfred Knapp | 27: Unidentified/St Catherine's College Library | 28–29: Antonio Gato | 30: The Jones Family 37: Royal Danish Library, the Art Library | 38–39: Bozhen Zhang | 40: Kelsey Moriarty | 44: *Punch* (1959) | 45: *Punch* (1959) | 46: Royal Danish Library, the Art Library | 47: Royal Danish Library, the Art Library | 48: Royal Danish Library, the Art Library | 49: Royal Danish Library, the Art Library | 50: © Mogens Juhl; VISDA | 52: Bridgeman Images | 53: Daily Sketch Rota/St Catherine's College Library | 55 top: Royal Danish Library, the Art Library | 55 bottom: Royal Danish Library, the Art Library | 56: Oxford Mail & Times Ltd/St Catherine's College Library | 58: Royal Danish Library, the Art Library | 59: Royal Danish Library, the Art Library | 60 top: © Bo Bojesen; VISDA | 60 bottom: Unidentified/St Catherine's College Library | 61: © Jørgen Mogensen; VISDA | 62: Surveyor to the University. The Malthouse, Tidmarsh Lane, Oxford | 64–65: Florence Baker Masters | 66: Florence Baker Masters | 71 (all): Mammoth.tv, London | 72: Mammoth.tv, London | 74–75: Flynn Hallman | 76: Kelsey Moriarty | 80: Royal Danish Library, the Art Library | 83: Royal Danish Library, the Art Library | 86–87: Royal Danish Library, the Art Library | 122 top: Unidentified/St Catherine's College Library | 123: Royal Danish Library, the Art Library | 124: Oxford Mail & Times Ltd/St Catherine's College Library | 128: Unidentified/St Catherine's College Library | 138: Royal Institute of British Architects; RIBA Collections | 142: St Catherine's College Library | 150: Royal Danish Library, the Art Library | 151 top: Royal Institute of British Architects; RIBA Collections | 151 middle: Peter Denney's private archive | 152–153: Forest Clevenger | 154: Amy Barnes | 175: Library, St Catherine's College | 180 left: The Surveyor to the University, The Malthouse, Oxford | 182–183: Kelsey Moriarty | 184: Forest Clevenger | 188 (series): *Catz Eye*; Michaelmas (6/1986) | 188 bottom left: *The Wheel*; Ingram Wilcox (1964) | 193: Royal Danish Library, the Art Library | 194: *Catz Eye* (3/1982) | 196–197: Matteo Flaviocatilo | 198: Daisy Connolly | 206: Unidentified/St Catherine's College Library | 207: St Catherine's College Library | 208–209: Shalini Ganendra | 210: Florence Baker Masters

For a small number of illustrations, it has not been possible to identify or contact the copyright holders. Any resulting copyright infringements are involuntary and unintended. Any outstanding rightful copyright claims will be remunerated as if a prior agreement had been made.

Literature

A tree's journey through Oxford. (1964, 21 April). *Oxford Mail*.

Aalborg Amtstidende. (1956, 13 October). Skolebørn i luksusvillaer. *Aalborg Amtstidende*, 4.

Ainsworth, R., & Howell, C. (Eds.) (2012). *St Catherine's, Oxford: A pen portrait*. Third Millennium Publishing.

Archer, M. J. (1963) The New College. *The Wheel*, 24.

Arkitekt-kampagne mod Arne Jacobsen [Architects' campaign against Arne Jacobsen]. (1959, 25 February). *Politiken* 5, 11.

Arne Jacobsen accepterer [Arne Jacobsen accepts]. (1950, 7 April). *Politiken*, 12.

Arne Jacobsen: Absolut moderne [Arne Jacobsen: Absolutely modern]. (2002). *Louisiana Revy*, 43(1).

Arne Jacobsens Oxford [Arne Jacobsen's Oxford]. (1960, 28 October). *Politiken*, 1, 9.

Arne Jacobsen Buildings. (2010). Box LLC.

Bamber, R. H. (1963). Trinity Term. *The Wheel*, 1.

Banham, R. (1964). Criticism: St Catherine's College, Oxford, Churchill College, Cambridge. *The Architectural Review*, 136(811), 174–179, 180–187, 188–194.

Behind Glass. (1964, 24 July). *The Times, Educational Supplement*.

Bodelsen, A. (1963, 18 July). Arne Jacobsen i Oxford [Arne Jacobsen in Oxford]. *Berlingske Aftenavis*, 4.

Booth, D. (1960). St Catherine's College, Oxford. *The Builder*, 118(6129), 821–824.

Borders, W. (1979, 11 November). Another bastion falls to women: Oxford. *The New York Times*, 1, 22.

Bowman, A. (Ed.) (2002). *How to be modern: Arne Jacobsen in the 21st century*. Museum of Modern Art Oxford.

Brockman, H. A. N. (1964, 4 August). St Catherine's College, Oxford: A classical conception. *Financial Times*.

Brooks, P. (1984). *Reading for the plot. Design and intention in narrative*. Alfred A. Knopf.

Brown, J. (2000). *The modern garden*. Thames & Hudson.

Browne, K. (1977). Eyehold on Oxford... Combination of fine buildings into a townscape. *The Architectural Review*, 162(970), 341–349.

Bullock, A. (1984). *How St Catherine's College came to be founded* [A talk given to the Middle Common Room of St Catherine's College on 31 May 1984 by the Founding Master, Lord Bullock of Leafield; verbatim transcript].

Bygherren skal holde sin mund [The client should keep their mouth shut]. (1961, 5 September). *Politiken*, 9.

Carter, J. (1971, 17 November). *Architects' Journal Information Library*, 1105–1106.

College builders meet the demands of a perfectionist (1964, 30 July). *Building Industry News*.

Controversial St Catherine's College considered by a student of architecture. (1964, 22 October). *The Oxford Magazine*, 29–32.

Cooper, L. (2003). *The Gardens of St Catherine's College, Oxford: A review – with the future in mind* [draft dissertation].

Craig, S. P. (1995). *A guide to the gardens of St Catherine's College, Oxford*. St Catherine's College.

Dansk arkitekt bedømt i England [Danish architecture judged in England]. (1961, 18 January). *Demokraten*, 4.

Davies, K. (1997). Scandinavian Furniture in Britain: Finmar and the UK Market, 1949–1952. *Journal of Design History*, 10(1), 39–52.

Davies, M. (2002). *Margaret Davies talk for C20 Society-2002-Library architecture at Oxford-St Catherine's College*. Box LXIC: Talks by Lord Bullock and others: Oral history.

Davies, M., & Davies, D. (1997). *Creating St Catherine's College*. St Catherine's College.

de Coninck-Smith, N. (2010). Experts at work: A micro-study of architects and school buildings in Denmark, 1940–1970. In K. Petersen & Å. Lundqvist, *In experts we trust: Knowledge, politics and bureaucracy in Nordic welfare states* (pp. 223–248). Syddansk Universitetsforlag.

de Wit, S. (2018). *Hidden landscapes: The metropolitan garden as a multi-sensory expression of place*. Architectura & Natura.

Denney, P. (2024). *Working with Arne Jacobsen: Some personal impressions*. Kingsbury Publishing.

Dr. Jacobsen, I presume. (1968, 2 February). *Berlingske Tidende*, backpage.

Elizabeth fik diskret hjælp da hun murede [Elizabeth received discreet assistance when she tried her hand at bricklaying]. (1960, 5 November). Politiken, 1, 2.

Englands dronning ser dansk arkitektur [England's Queen sees Danish architecture]. (1960, 28 September). *Næstved Tidende*.

Esben Kvadersten arkitekt M.A.A. [Esben Kvadersten, architect (MAA)] (1959). *Arkitekten*, 61(20), 364.

Faber, T. (1968). *Arne Jacobsen*. Tiranti.

Fälling, C. (1964, 26 July). Moderne dansk arkitektur og engelsk tradition [Modern Danish architecture and English tradition]. *Berlingske Tidende*, Section 2, 7.

Frewer, L. & Gouk, P. (1974). *St Catherine's Year: Oxford 1977*. St Catherine's College.

Gardiner, S. Changing Masterpiece. *The Observer*. [Box 8_Magazine articles]

Gibbons, R. E. (1961). Trinity Term, 1961. *The Wheel*, 1.

Green, P. (2012). Memoirs of an idle labourer – or how I built my own college. In R. Ainsworth & C. Howell (Eds.), *St Catherine's, Oxford: A Pen Portrait* (pp. 161–164). Third Millennium Publishing.

Gregory, R. (2004). Teaching an Old Cat New Tricks. *The Architectural Review*, 215(1284), 74–79.

Grigs, D. (1966, 22 June). Encaenia in Oxford. *Oxford Mail*, front page.

Hartmann-Petersen, J. (1964, 24 July). Jacobsen of Oxford. *Politiken*, 9–10.

Harlang, C. (2005). *Danske designere: Knud Holscher* [Danish designers: Knud Holscher]. Aschehoug.

Harling, R. (1959, 1 March). Was Professor Jacobsen's journey really necessary? *The Sunday Times*, 33.

Hicks, M. (2004). Integrating women at Oxford and Harvard, 1964–1977. In L. Ulrich (Ed.), *Gender in Harvard and Radcliffe history*. Palgrave Macmillan.

Hodder, S. R. (2002). History: Jacobsen reconsidered. *Architecture Today*, (131), 54–56, 58, 61.

Home? (1985). *Catz Eye*, 4–5.

Jackson, S. (2002). Oxford's 'Best Motel': The dining room at St Catherine's College, Oxford. *Architectural Design*, 72(4), 22–25.

Jacobsen, A., Holscher, K., Arup, O., Balslev, M., Northcroft, Neighbour & Nicholson, Lankester, J., Lockton, P. J., Steensen Varming Mulcahy, Petersen, J., & Marshall-Andrew and Company Limited (1964). St Catherine's College, Oxford. *Official Architecture and Planning*, 27(9), 1067, 1069, 1071.

Jeannerat, P. (1960, 28 October) Among Oxford spires: A new sardine tin. *Daily Mail*, 9.

Jordan, R. F. (1959, 8 March). Awakening of the Dons. *The Observer*, 18.

Juniper, B. (1969–1970). The Garden of St Catherine's College, Oxford. *St Catherine's Chronicle, Oxford*, 14–15.

Juniper, B. (1980). A guide to the gardens of St Catherine's College, Oxford. St Catherine's College.

Kongelig begivenhed for Arne Jacobsen [Royal event for Arne Jacobsen]. (1960, 28 September). *Dagens Nyheder*.

Kromann-Andersen, E. (1994). Åben-plan skoler – fortid og fremtid [Open-plan schools – past and future]. In *Uddannelseshistorie* (pp. 73–88). Selskabet for Dansk Skolehistorie.

Kural, R. (2018). *The town hall at the edge of the forest: About Søllerød Town Hall designed by Arne Jacobsen and Flemming Lassen*. Forlaget Rhodos.

Lack, A. (2009, September). New role for St Cross. *Oxfordshire Limited Edition*, 77, 79.

Lax, J. (1964, 14 November). Oxford Ziggurats: New Architecture. *Isis*, 16–20.

Léger, J.-M. (2013). Arne Jacobsen: Le College Ste Catherine à Oxford 1959–1964 [Arne Jacobsen: St Catherine's College at Oxford 1959–1964]. *Moniteur Architecture AMC*.

Macdonald, K. (1963). The Birth of a College. *The Wheel*, 28–29.

Makaber demonstration mod Arne Jacobsen [Macabre demonstration against Arne Jacobsen]. (1959, 4 March). *Social-Demokraten*, 3.

Malkiel, N. W. (2016). *'Keep the Damned Women Out': The Struggle for Coeducation*. Princeton University Press.

Malmquist, O. (1963, 5 December). 100 på toppen. *Aktuelt*, 18.

Man må bøje sig for Jacobsen [Credit is due to Jacobsen]. (1966, 16–17 July). *Information*.

Manden er sikkert smøgforlegen... [The man is probably craving a cigarette]. (1966, 23 June). *Politiken*, 14.

Manser, M. (1964, 26 July). The Oxbridge Double. *The Observer*.

Mentze, E. (1959, 19 April). Teknik og aandfuldt haandværk samles i St. Catherine's College [Technology and spirited artisanship come together in St Catherine's College]. *Berlingske Tidende*, 17–18.

Møller, H. S. (1971, 25 March). Arne Jacobsen død midt i sit arbejde [Arne Jacobsen died in the midst of his work]. *B.T.*, 4.

Møller, P. (1960, 28 October). Stormen blæser op mod Arne Jacobsen [Arne Jacobsen facing strong headwinds]. *B.T.*, back page.

Møller, V. A. (2019). *Dansk arkitektur i 1960'erne* [Danish architecture during the 1960s]. Forlaget Rhodos.

Mr Macmillan praises a great Dane. (1964, 17 October). *The Guardian*.

Myerson, J. (1988, 6 May). The Art of Arne Jacobsen. *Design Week*. [Box 8_9_15 Magazine articles]

Nabokov, V. (1955). *Lolita*. Putnam.

Nielsen, J. A. (1964, 24 July). Ikke en dansker, men Arne Jacobsen [Not a Dane but Arne Jacobsen]. *Politiken*, 10.

Ninka (1971, 28 February). Det nye kritiseres altid [New ideas are always criticised]. *Politiken*, p. 13.

Ørskov, W. (1987). *Den åbne skulptur*. Borgen.

Oxford-grundstenen fjernet i trillebør af tre studerende [Oxford foundation stone removed in wheelbarrow by three students]. (1960, 6 November). *Politiken*, 4.

Out of the Air. (1964, 20 August). *The Listener*, 270.

Parkhouse, G. (1964, 24 July). All his own work. *Daily Mail*.

Pedersen, J. (1964). Arne Jacobsen i Oxford [Arne Jacobsen in Oxford]. In *Gutenberghus Årsskrift*.

Pevsner, N. (1943). *An outline of European architecture*. Penguin.

Plougsgaard, H. (2012, 4 August). Danske spor i Oxford [Danish traces in Oxford]. *Morgenavisen Jyllands-Posten*.

Purcell (2017). *Student accommodation and graduate centre St Catherine's College: Design and access statement*. Purcell.

Ramaskriget om St. Catherine's College i Oxford [The outcry at St. Catherine's College in Oxford]. (1959). *Arkitekten*, 61(7), 128–129.

Randall, A. (1959, 24 March). Traditioner i Oxford [Traditions at Oxford]. *Berlingske Tidende*, 14.

Rosenfield, R. (1964, 24 July). Field wanted. *Oxford Mail*, 3.

Rosenfield, R. (1964, 24 July). The Master's home suits his wife. *Oxford Mail*, 3.

Rosser, G. (2021, 4 March). The icon of St Catherine in the library. [Talk for the Senior Common Room].

Rowntree, D. (1964, 24 July). Ordered simplicity. *The Guardian*.

Rowntree, D. (1965, 23 June). The beauty of repetition. *The Guardian*.

Russell, J. (1964, 26 July). The master builder. *The Sunday Times*, 6–12.

Sådan siger de andre [What the others are saying] (1961). *Arkitekten*, 63(1), A26, A 28.

Schulz, E. (1966, 30 July). St. Catherine's und andere Colleges: Traditionen in Beton [St Catherine's and other colleges: Traditions in concrete]. *Frankfurter Allgemeine Zeitung*, (174).

Sestoft, J. (1991). Arne Jacobsen and the Nordic aspect. In *Arne Jacobsen*. Aarhus School of Architecture and Dansk Arkitektur og Byggeeksport Center.

Sheridan, M. (2023). *Room 606: The SAS house and the work of Arne Jacobsen*. Strandberg Publishing.

Sherwood, J., & Pevsner, N. (1974). *Buildings of England: Oxfordshire*. Penguin.

Skriver, P. E. (1961). St. Catherine's College, Oxford. *Arkitekten*, (1), 3–7.

Skriver, P. E. (1965). St. Catherine's College i Oxford [St Catherine's College in Oxford]. *Arkitektur*, 1, 1–40.

Skriver, P. E. (1982). Arne Jacobsens St. Catherine's [Arne Jacobsen's St Catherine's]. *Arkitektur*, 2, 41–43.

Snow, C. P. (1959). *The two cultures and the scientific revolution*. The Syndics of the Cambridge University Press.

'So what if it's ugly and uncomfortable – it's important'. (1993, 7 April). *The Independent*.

Soares, J. A. (1999). *The decline of privilege: The modernization of Oxford University*. Stanford University Press.

Solaguren-Beascoa, F. (1991). *Clásicos del Diseño: Arne Jacobsen*. Santa & Cole.

Solaguren-Beascoa, F. (2002). 1960–1964 St Catherine's College, Manor Road, Oxford (Great Britain). In *Arne Jacobsen: Approach to his complete works 1950–1971*, vol. 2 (pp. 182–195). The Danish Architectural Press.

Soto, A. (2021). *A certain logic of expectations*. The Eriskay Connection.

St Catherine's College, Oxford. (1964, 5 August). *Architects' Journal*, 323–342.

St Catherine's College, Oxford. (1964, September). *Architectural Design*, 435, 440–441.

St Catherine's College, Oxford (1964, September–October). *Interior Design*, 261–269.

St Catherine's College, Oxford: Official Opening, Friday, October 16th, 1964: Seating plan. (1964, 16 October).

St Catherine's College, Oxford: The year 2015. St Catherine's College.

St Catherine's first students. (1962, 12 October). *Oxford Times*.

St Cross Church, Holywell: Its history, architecture, people, and conversion into an Historic Collections Centre (2011). Balliol College Oxford.

St Hill, C. (2012). It is 50 years since St Catherine's, the youngest of the Oxford University colleges, was designed by Arne Jacobsen. *Blueprint*, (318), 29.

Suzuki, T. (2014). *Arne Jacobsen: Jacobsen no kenchiku to design* [Jacobsen's Architecture and Design]. TOTO Publishing.

Thau, C., & Vindum, K. (1998). *Arne Jacobsen*. Arkitektens Forlag.

The old and mellow colleges of Oxford meet a long, low concrete stranger. (1960, October). *Daily Express*.

Translation of a Motto. (1964/65). *Esso Magazine*, 14(1), 13–15. 9 [Box 9_6_More Press Cuttings].

Treasures from a Modern Oxford Archive. (2019). St Catherine's College.

Trench, B. (1967). Come Again. *The Wheel*, 37–38.

Trotman, R. R., & Garrett, E. J. K. (1962). *The non-collegiate students and St Catherine's Society 1868–1962*. Oxford University Press.

Tyack, G. (1998). *Oxford: An architectural guide*. Oxford University Press.

University of Oxford Annual Admissions Statistical Report, 2022. (2022). University of Oxford.

Wakisaka, K. (2021). Arne Jacobsen and St Catherine's College: Traditions defined by modernism. *Approach*, 4–23.

Webb, M. (1966, 17. February). A jewel amid the dreaming spires. *Country Life*, 348–350.

Young, B. A. (1959, 4 March). The Catherine squeal: Should Danish architects be allowed to design Oxford colleges? *Punch*, 318–319.

Zietzschmann, E. (1965). Saint Catherine's College in Oxford. *Bauen + Wohnen = Construction + habitation = Building + home: internationale Zeitschrift*, (7), 281–294.

TV and film

Evergreens & nevergreens: Arne Jacobsen 100 years. (2002). Danish Design Centre.

Dexter, C., Lewis, R. (Writers), Pearce, A. (Director). (2017, 8 January). Game (Season 4, Episode 1) [TV series episode]. In Eaton, R., Lewis, R., & Timmer, D. (Executive producers). *Endeavour*. ITV.

Dreyer, O. (Director). (1970). *Arne Jacobsen i Oxford* [Arne Jacobsen in Oxford] [TV documentary]. DR.

Hausner, J. (Director). (2023). *Club Zero*. Coop99 Filmproduktion.

Øhlenschlæger, S. E. (Editor), & Pedersen, L. A. (Writer). (2003). *Arne Jacobsen: Arkitekt og designer* [Arne Jacobsen: Architect and designer]. DR.

Torp, L. R. (Producer). (2021). *Arne Jacobsens moderne Danmark* [Arne Jacobsen's modern Denmark] [TV documentary]. DR.

Index

A

Aalto, Alvar 44
Aberdeen, David du R 21
Accommodation blocks 82
Aesthetic tyranny 185, 192
AJ Oxford table lamp 112
Alan Bullock Building 180
Amphitheatre 139, 144
Architects' Co-Partnership (ACP) 56–57
Arup, Ove 21, 24, 124

B

Back to the Future 206
Baistow, Tom 9, 185, 206
Balliol College 67, 148
Bamber, R. H. 203
Banham, Reyner 61, 93, 159, 162
Bell tower 93, 124, 128
Bellagio 26
Bells, Japanese 128
Bernard Sunley Lecture Theatre 101
Bernard Sunley Building 58, 82, 101–102, 132, 180, 190
Bike shed 93, 147
Blinds 170, 175, 199
Bo, Jørgen 21
Bodelsen, Anders 61–62, 192
Bodleian Library 190
Borthwick, Thomas 123
Bowra, Maurice 24
Braddell, Darcy 44
Brasenose 56, 71
Brasenose College 57
Bricks 132
Brooks, Peter 72
Brutalism 132
Bryan-Brown, A. N. 51
Bullock, Alan 20–21, 26–27, 35–36, 45, 47, 53, 62, 123, 142, 147–149, 168, 175, 193, 203, 206

C

Campbell, Mia 41, 203
Canterbury Cathedral 44
Carver, M. J. 175
Cats 189
Catz Eye 194
Cedar tree 138–139
Chapel 148–149
Christ Church 17, 67
Christensen, Kai 24
Churchill College 18, 162
Clevenger, Forest 152
Concert Hall 93
Cooper, Louise 144
Coulthurst, Jessie B. 148–149
Coupled windows 175

D

Danish Building Centre 21, 23–24
Davies, Derek 18, 149
Davies, Margaret 18
De Coninck-Smith, Ning 36
Denney, Peter 9, 56, 138, 176, 206
Dickinson, Andrew 164
Dining Hall 82, 106–112
Dissing+Weitling 176
Dixey, Michael 150–151
Double glazing 175
Dowson, Philip 24, 50

E

Elevations and Choice of Architects Committee 21, 24
Elizabeth II 53
Endeavour 70, 162
English Heritage 56, 193
English Heritage (Historic England) 176, 189
Entz night 185
Esso Petroleum Company (Exxon) 58

F

Facade renovation 176
Fisher, Norman 21
Fitness centre 67
Flaviocatilo, Matteo 196
Foulds, Adam 175
Functional Traditionalism 35, 45
Furnishings 192

G

Ganendra, Dame Shalini Amerasinghe 208
Garden City Movement 62
Garden plan 138, 142, 147
Gardens, semi-private 139
Gato, Antonio 28
Gender policies 165, 168
Gesamtkunstwerk 61, 114
Gibbs, James 190
Gouk, Penelope 170
Gowan, James 21
Graduate Centre 180–181
Green, Peter 132
Gropius, Walter 44

H

Hallman, Flynn 74
Hausner, Jessica 72
Hawksmoor, Nicholas 21
Helen Gaskin Memorial Garden 143
Henningsen, Poul 50
Hepworth, Barbara 114, 147, 203
High Table 41, 113
Historic England (English Heritage) 176
Hodder Associates 180–181
Hodder, Stephen 181
Hodgson, R. B. C. 150
Holden, Ben 152
Holscher, Knud 24, 81, 143, 150, 181, 193
Holywell Church 148
Holywell Great Meadow 17, 53
Holywell North Stream 175, 181
Honorary doctorate, Arne Jacobsen's 51

I

Isaac Wolfson Trustees 24

J

Jeannerat, Pierre 10
Johnson-Marshall, Stirrat 21
Jones, Biba 30, 203
Jordan, Robert Furneaux 45
Junior Common Room (JCR) 31, 54, 58, 114, 139, 155, 185, 190, 192, 199, 203, 211
Juniper, Barrie 138–139, 142–143, 193

K

Kempis, Thomas à 194
Khakurel, Asmod 184, 203
King, Augusta Ada 70
Knudsen, Sidse Babett 72
Koppel, Eva and Nils 21, 23

L

Lake Como 26
Lankester, Jack 21, 47, 62, 132, 181, 189
Larsen, Martin Alfosin 64, 203
Lasdun, Denys 21
Le Corbusier 44, 70
Lecture Theatre (Bernard Sunley Building) 58, 82, 101–102, 132, 180, 190
Library 82, 96, 155
Lovelace College 70
Loyola, Ignatius of 194

218

M

Macmillan, Harold 51, 58
Malkiel, Nancy Weiss 165
Mandelson, Peter 193
Manser, Michael 162
Marble 132
Mary Sunley Building 180
Master's house 93, 124, 155
Masters, Florence Baker 64, 198, 203
Materials 132
Matriculation Day 72, 164
McMillan, Jake 203, 210
Men of the Year (1959): Alan Bullock and Arne Jacobsen 44
Merton College 17, 150–151, 181
Middle Common Room (MCR) 58, 155, 181, 203
Modernism 35, 132
Møller, C. F. 21, 23
Moriarty, Kelsey 76, 182, 203
Mulholland, Marc 159
Munkegaard School 23, 35–37
Music House 121–124, 149

N

New College 168
Non-collegiate students 17, 20
Nordic Modernism 35
Nova et Vetera (St Catherine's motto) 56, 190

O

Old Clarendon 17
Oriel College 168
Oxford Preservation Trust Award 123
Oxford's best motel 159, 163

P

Pedersen, Johan 56
Pevsner, Nikolaus 192
Phillips, Tom 31, 112
Plot 70, 72
Porter's Lodge 129
Powell & Moya Architect Practice 21, 56–57
Powers, Michael 57
Prince Philip, Duke of Edinburgh 53
Princess Margaret 101, 123
Purcell 93, 151, 180–181

Q

Quadrangle (Quad) 31, 41, 49, 67, 86, 93, 139, 143, 145, 155, 199, 203, 211
Queen Elizabeth II 53

R

RAAC (Reinforced Autoclaved Aerated Concrete) 206
Radcliffe Camera 56, 190
Reid, John and Sylvia 21
RIBA (Royal Institute of British Architects) 24, 44, 51
Richardson, Albert 47
River Cherwell 17, 53, 82, 123
Rockefeller Foundation 26, 149
Room C 102
Rosenberg & Mardall 21
Royal Institute of British Architects (RIBA) 24, 44, 51

S

Sandstone 132
SAS building (SAS Royal Hotel, Copenhagen) 48, 61–62
Senior Common Room (SCR) 54, 58, 114, 118, 139, 155, 190
Sens, William of 44
Sergeant, Harriet 170
Sestoft, Jørgen 35
Sharp, Thomas 62
Shaw Room 102
Sheldonian Theatre 53, 164
Shepherd-Barr, Kirsten 164
Sheppard, Richard 61
Sherwood, Jennifer 192
Shewan, Rodney 123
Simopoulos, John Charalambos 193
Slate 132
Smithson, Alison and Peter 21
Snow, Charles Percy 26
Soto, Arturo 191
Spence, Basil 24
Sports ground 150–151
Sports pavilion 123
St Aldate's 17
St Catherine's Society 17
St Catherine's Wheel 189
St Cross 148
St John's College 56–57
Steensen & Varming 176
Stirling, James 21
Structuralism 132
Student rebellion 165
Student accommodation 55, 162–163, 170, 173, 180, 190, 199

T

Tapestries, Dining Hall 31
The Wheel 189
Thames 143, 175
Trench, Barney 190
Trinity College 23, 67
Tsurigane 128
Tutor's office 159
Twentieth Century Society 176

U

University of Strathclyde, Glasgow 51
Utzon, Jørn 21, 23

V

Van Es, Bart 159
Vanbrugh, John 21
Villa Serbelloni 26

W

Waade, Ellen 176
Walzer, Richard 114
Wegner, Hans J. 50
Wenden, D. J. 150
Weylandt, Teit 176
Whitamore, Sybil Mary 122–123
Wilcox, Ingram 188
Wohlert, Vilhelm 21
Wolden-Ræthinge, Anne (Ninka) 170
Women's Liberation 165
Womersley, David 159
Worcester College 41
Wren, Christopher 21

Y

Yorke Rosenberg Mardall 21

Z

Zhang, Bozhen 38

About the author and the photographer

RENÉ KURAL (b. 1959)

PhD, architect (MAA); appointed co-director of Work Programme Sports and Leisure, Union Internationale des Architectes (UIA), Paris; former guest professor at Tokyo Institute of Technology and Tokyo University of Science, Japan; former head of centre, associate professor, researcher and lecturer at the Royal Danish Academy.

EDUCATION:

1987: MA (architecture), Royal Danish Academy, School of Architecture
1994: PhD, Royal Danish Academy, School of Architecture
2002: Approved as associate professor, Royal Danish Academy, School of Architecture
2018: Leadership training programme 'Ledelse i kreative vidensvirksomheder' (Leadership in creative knowledge companies; LKVV)

SPECIALTY AREAS:

As a writer, René Kural aims to place significant buildings and urban planning into new architectural, political, or journalistic contexts. His work establishes new architectural connections between architecture, context, and setting. A key topic of his research is the synergy between healthy cities and 'the good life', which he seeks to promote by influencing Danish urban planning through his work. To this end, he has engaged in research, communication, advisory, and development tasks and projects for Danish and foreign architecture firms as well as local governments, public authorities, and foundations.

PREVIOUS PUBLICATIONS (SELECTED):

Kural, R. (2018). *The Town Hall at the Edge of the Forest: About Søllerød Town Hall designed by Arne Jacobsen and Flemming Lassen*
Forlaget Rhodos, ISBN 9788779990173.
Danish edition same year, ISBN 9788779990203.

Kural, R. (2012). *OUT! Om Dansk Tennis Club og tennispilleren Leif Rovsing*
[OUT! About the Danish Tennis Club and the tennis player Leif Rovsing]
Forlaget Rhodos, ISBN 9788772459912.

Kural, R. (1999). *Playing Fields: Alternative Spaces for Sports, Culture, and Recreation*
Kunstakademiets Arkitektskoles Forlag, ISBN 9788787136368.
Danish edition same year, ISBN 9788787136341.

Kural, R. (2000). *Architecture of the Information Society*.
Kunstakademiets Arkitektskoles Forlag, ISBN 9788787136295.
Danish edition 1995, ISBN 9788787136120.

RASMUS HJORTSHØJ (b. 1979)

Photographer, architect (MAA), PhD. Independent photographer specialising in representations of the built environment. In a separate practice, COAST, Rasmus Hjortshøj also conducts research into architecture and representation with a particular focus on coastal territories during the Anthropocene.

EDUCATION:

2002: Skolen for Billedkunst (School of Visual Arts), Aarhus
2008: MA (architecture), Aarhus School of Architecture
2021: PhD, Aarhus School of Architecture

SPECIALTY AREAS:

Rasmus Hjortshøj's work provides a precise and sensuous representation of the built environment that draws on his experience as a practising architect. In collaboration with leading Nordic architecture and design studios and institutions, Rasmus Hjortshøj's practice revolves around the representation of new works of architecture, cultural heritage, and landscaping. His research activities are based on so-called territorial photography, which combines documentation with an aesthetic framing of mainly urbanised coastal areas. These studies range from the immediate local sphere to the wider territorial interconnectedness of nature and culture and aim to shed new light on how architecture shapes and is shaped by the territories it occupies.

PREVIOUS PUBLICATIONS (SELECTED):

Weiss, K. L. (2022). *New Danish Architecture: 10 Buildings, 10 Architects, 10 Themes*.
Photographs by Rasmus Hjortshøj, 944 pages. Strandberg Publishing, ISBN 9788794102292.

Hjortshøj, R. (2021). *Det sammenfiltrede territorie: Repræsentation af det danske urbaniserede kystterritorie i Antropocæn igennem fotografi* [Territory of entanglement: Representation of the Danish urbanised coastal territory in the Anthropocene through photography].
PhD dissertation, Aarhus School of Architecture.

Weiss, K. L. (Ed.) (2021). *Gellerup*. [English edition].
Photographs by Rasmus Hjortshøj et al., 411 pages. Danish Architectural Press, ISBN 978874074632
Danish edition same year, ISBN 9788774074625.
Cirelli, J. (Ed.) (2021).

Our Urban Living Room: Learning from Copenhagen (3rd edition, 1st edition published 2016). Photographs by Rasmus Hjortshøj et al. Arvinius+Orfeus, ISBN 9789187543395.

Weiss, K. L. (Ed.). (2022). *BLOX*.
Photographs by Rasmus Hjortshøj. Realdania, ISBN 9788792230973.
Danish edition same year, ISBN 9788792230966.

Acknowledgements

It was my great pleasure to meet Knud Holscher[271] and Peter Denney from Arne Jacobsen's architecture firm, who were Jacobsen's on-site project architects for St Catherine's during the early 1960s. I thank them both for their loyal support and positive contributions.

At St Catherine's College, Master Kersti Börjars welcomed me with open arms, as did librarian Barbara Costa, Margaret Davies, and former Home Bursar James Bennett. They all generously shared their vast knowledge with me. The students and my colleagues at the college were a huge source of inspiration, for which I am profoundly grateful.

Many thanks to the entire team behind the publication: first of all, Arne Jacobsen's grandson Tobias Jacobsen, who planted the seed for this book, as well as editor Lil Vad-Schou, photographer Rasmus Hjortshøj, graphic designer Søren Varming – the grandson of Jørgen Varming, who was one of the founders of Steensen & Varming, the consulting engineers involved in the construction of St Catherine's College – translator Dorte Herholdt Silver, copy editor Sarah Quigley and publisher Lars Erik Strandberg.

Director Irene Houstrup Madsen, art historian Annika Skaarup Larsen, and Viktoria Larsen of Arne Jacobsen Design I/S provided helpful and professional guidance to Arne Jacobsen's sketches.

Thanks to Professor Martin Zerlang for his constructive criticism of the manuscript, page by page, and for offering inspiring professional insights that enhanced the book.

Finally, my thanks go to the archives at St Catherine's College; the Royal Institute of British Architects (RIBA); the Royal Danish Library, including the Art Library (the Architecture Collection in Søborg); the Danish National Archives; the library at the Royal Danish Academy; and other Danish and English libraries, for the many hours I have spent in your inspiring, welcoming, learned, and educational company.

271) Harlang, C. (2005). *Danske designere: Knud Holscher*. Aschehoug.

Catz

St Catherine's College
by Arne Jacobsen

Strandberg Publishing A/S
Gammel Mønt 14
DK – 1117 Copenhagen K
Denmark

www.strandbergpublishing.dk

© 2024 René Kural and Strandberg Publishing
With photographs by Rasmus Hjortshøj

The work is peer-reviewed
The certification means that an independent peer of at least PhD level has made a written assessment justifying this book's scientific quality and original contribution.

The book was made possible by the generous support of Copydan's Autorkonto and the Danish Arts Foundation.

Editor:
Lil Vad-Schou

Translator:
Dorte Herholdt Silver

Copy editor:
Sarah Quigley

Illustrations:
See credits on page 215

Graphic design and cover design:
Søren Varming MDD, Punktum Design

Image processing:
Narayana Press, Gylling

Typeface:
Nuacht Serif Text and Sans Regular
by Henrik Kubel, A2–Type, London

Paper:
150g Arctic Volume White

Printing and binding:
Livonia Print, Riga

Printed in Latvia 2024
1st edition, 1st print run
ISBN 978-87-94418-26-3

Copying from this book may only take place at institutions that have entered into agreement with Copydan and only within the terms and conditions set down in said agreement.